55 Myths, Tips & Secrets

Bend's Essential Guide to Landscaping

Fred Swisher & Sarah Whipple

Published by
Incubation Press
Bend, OR 97701
866-839-BOOK

55 Myths, Tips & Secrets: Bend's Essential Guide to Landscaping

2nd Edition May 2008

Edited by
Linden Gross
Bend, OR 97701

Printed in the United States of America

I dedicate this book to my mom and dad, and to my grandmother, Marguerite Whipple, who guided me in discovering the wonder, beauty and wisdom of nature.

– Sarah

Acknowledgments

We often hear how good work wasn't done by one person alone. Sometimes that can seem a bit overly dramatic. In my case this book simply would not have been possible without local writing coach Linden Gross. After struggling with writing for the last ten years, finding and working with her on this book has been a dream come true for me. Thanks Linden.

The other realization I had while writing this book is how I really got my start in landscaping in the first place. While I was growing up in Seattle, my dad, a manager at Boeing, loved building rockeries and being out in nature. He influenced all three of his sons. My brother Bob now works a few steps away from Dad's Boeing office. My other brother, Dave, following Dad's second career, has built a commercial real estate and development business. Rebel that I am, I picked what dad loved to do while he was not working, as my "alternative" to a career. At the critical age of fourteen, he found me my first landscape job at Sunriver. Following this passion for beautiful landscapes turned into a real career after all. Thanks, Dad.

– *Fred*

I don't divide architecture, landscape and gardening; to me they are one.

Luis Barragan
World-renowned architect

Contents

Dear Reader:

I grew up in Bend when the word *development* sounded foreign. It was a great place to fish, hunt and climb mountains. People here were mill workers, loggers and farmers. There were just a few merchants and virtually zero art or culture.

Since then just about everything has changed – especially when it comes to Bend's landscapes. Even as recently as the late eighties, using boulders and rock in landscapes was considered weird. Water features only got popular after the mid nineties. Landscaping here continues to change considerably more than building design, with craftsman style homes circa 1950 still popular and very few homes oriented for solar gain.

I've heard it said that leadership is mileage. One thousand local landscapes ago, I got my start by building berms for Bo Sherby at Sunriver in the summer of 1970. I was fourteen. Over the years, I've learned contracting and design. In college I majored in art and business, and studied landscaping and architecture. I became a good carpenter during those years too. After college I worked in New York's World Trade Center on the floor of the New York Mercantile exchange. It was exciting and, after a while, lucrative enough. But living in Manhattan wasn't for me. I longed for creative natural projects. So I moved back to Oregon and apprenticed at tile-setting for Eugene Tile in 1987. Later I worked as a licensed building contractor doing remodeling. Soon I was building a progressive prototype home for the one of the early developers of Sunriver, my dad Don Swisher. In the early nineties, I invested in heavy equipment and started providing sculptural landscaping and excavation services in Bend. Our tree and shrub nursery, Bend Pine Nursery, got its start soon after that. The focus has since shifted even more toward education and innovative design.

Over the years, I've visited thousands of landscape projects and dozens of national and international botanical gardens. Since 1995, I've worked as a landscape design consultant. I've seen and been involved in hundreds of people's design decisions. During the nineties—when I had many people working for my company—we landscaped as many as seventy tract homes at a time (e.g. the Wishing Well subdivision). We did underground utilities and excavating for developments (e.g. Higher Ground). We even built the sets and landscape for an ABC-TV mini-series ("McKenna").

I've downscaled the business since then, but I still love a landscape challenge. Lately, with only a small crew, we completed a job in just thirty consecutive days that others weren't able to finish over a period of six months. Our clients were stunned and relieved to have a lovely landscape they could finally enjoy.

I prefer to landscape larger residences with a natural style or homes with water nearby. But these last years we've done car dealerships (e.g. Robberson Ford), as well as light industrial, farms and offices. Even after all this time, the projects keep getting better and more inspiring. At fifty-one, my body doesn't have the stamina it once did, but experience over the years has taught me how to streamline and simplify the work, which makes for "A" caliber landscapes.

These last twelve years as a local seminar promoter, I've worked with many famous speakers, best-selling authors, and business gurus. January 1996 was our first major event with Tony Robbins' teacher Jim Rohn. Other classes and seminars followed, with famous names like Dr. Wayne Dyer, Dr. Deepak Chopra, Michael Gerber (author of the *E-Myth*), Michael Basch (Fed Ex co-founder) and Robert Allen (author of *Nothing Down*).

If you've been attending our most recent events, you've probably noticed a Chinese influence. In 2004, I got to tour a couple dozen of China's famous gardens and temples in Suzhou and Shanghai, which inspired me to bring a Chinese sensibility to my work. In 2005, landscape architect David Vala presented "Gardens of China." In 2006, our "Masters of China" event included Master George Xu, Master David Leung and Master Yun Yin Sen. My love for Chinese gardens (and martial arts) inspired me to return to China in 2007.

As this book is being completed, we are sponsoring a two-day water-feature class that includes a hands-on "lab," in which a small, cutting-edge swimming pond with a waterfall and natural filtration gets completed and installed by the group.

As a professional speaker and a lifelong learner, my purpose in writing this book is to improve—and provide valuable and innovative—landscape knowledge. The right input really does yield results, a lesson I learned firsthand in high school. One day during a high school track meet, I got coached in high jump by another school's track coach. I had already been doing the western roll for almost the whole season. But that day, I followed the formula the new coach taught me and after a few minutes of practice I jumped a full six inches higher than ever before! Half-a-foot was more than enough extra height for me to earn a first-place medal for the first time that season. Not only did I win that day, but for the rest of the season I jumped at the new level.

Over the years of running two very different businesses (landscaping and seminars), I've also learned that it takes a formula to have a successful system. Part of *my* formula is working with my co-author and life partner Sarah Whipple. Sarah brings her passion, her attention to detail, and her love of nature to this book and her work. She's an experienced manager of Bend Pine Nursery, an art therapist, a fire-walk instructor and a master gardener. I've never met anyone in my life who shares more hugs and laughter with her clients.

The other part of our success formula is you! Your questions, comments and concerns make Sarah and me better providers. By keeping the process as alive as the subject itself, we stay up to date, relevant, and informed. We can't be successful unless we can help you with your ideas, challenges and projects. Your feedback and referrals make up our successful formula.

Thank you!

Fred Swisher

Dear Reader,

If you're lucky in life you discover your true purpose. I was fortunate enough to find my calling seven years ago. A friend of mine had a small tree nursery he was moving and needed a place to put his inventory. I volunteered my yard and discovered I was a natural at working with—and caring for—the trees and plants. I loved it and have been working in the nursery and landscaping business ever since. After a couple years, I became the manager of Bend Pine Nursery. Today I am a green-industry certified Master Gardener. I love to study and learn all I can about trees and plants and how they grow, as well as what will grow here in Central Oregon.

In my youth, I would not have ever thought I would be planting trees and landscaping, but looking back on my life it all makes perfect sense. My family spent summers at "The Cabin"—a log cabin my great grandfather built on the shore of Lake Michigan in Door County, Wisconsin. I credit my grandmother and my dad for teaching me about nature and the woods. My grandma took me on hikes and taught me how to identify wildflowers, trees and other plants. My dad taught me how to camp and survive in the wilderness, to respect the earth, water, trees, animals, and to appreciate the beauty of nature.

When I was about eight or nine years old, my dad gave me a tree not too far from our cabin. I think I fell in love with trees right then. The tree was a great big, old white pine tree, with a big, fat branch just high enough to see above the underbrush and look out on the lake. My dad nailed steps on the trunk, so I could climb up and sit and daydream. That tree was my friend.

I moved to the West Coast in my twenties, and attended the University of Washington in Seattle, where I received a BA in Fine Art. Then I moved to Santa Fe, New Mexico for graduate school, where I got my Masters Degree in Art Therapy. Making art really amounts to problem-solving and finding a way to communicate and express oneself using painting drawing, sculpture, etc. Now that I work with trees and landscaping, I use the same creative process; only the canvas has changed. Today my pallet consists of trees, plants, flowers, rocks, and so on. I am still creating. My art and art-therapy background benefits my clients when I help them design beautiful, natural landscapes.

When I am in tune with myself I know my true purpose is working with trees, and teaching people about these life forms and how to care for them. My philosophy about nature is close to that of the native peoples of the world: I believe in Mother Earth and Father Sky and that we are all children of these parents. Whether we're people, animals, plants, trees, or fish, we are all here together, connected, relying on each other and on the earth and sky to live. The Native Americans consider trees to be a race of beings, a tribe. They call them "the one-leggeds." I love that.

When I plant trees, I know I'm helping the environment, since trees and plants make such an important contribution to the global ecosystem and the lives of human beings. Trees give so much: wood, heat, shelter, shade, beauty. They are the lungs of the earth, just as algae and water plants are the lungs of the oceans. I read once that a mature tree can supply enough oxygen for four people for life. It is my great honor and privilege to work with these magnificent beings. There are days when I'm hot, sweaty, and dirty from planting all day and my job doesn't seem so sublime. But in my heart, I know this is my gift to pass along. Doing this work is a way of sharing the love and knowledge I have for trees and landscaping, and the enjoyment of nature and the great outdoors we have here in Central Oregon.

Trees, plants, digging in the dirt and growing things make people happy. I believe that nature connects us to ourselves and to spirit. People want and need the ability to retreat into nature in their own back yards. I help them achieve that.

Sarah Whipple

PART 1

THE HARDSCAPE

Chapter 1

Landscape for Success

Creating a stunning landscape isn't accidental. Great results flow from good decisions and the best decisions are educated ones. In other words, being well informed as you start your landscape project will pay off. Before you get bogged down in the traps and the pitfalls of landscaping in Central Oregon, take a little time to get yourself up to speed. Many people confuse project results with luck or money. This book is a tool to help you avoid that mistake, along with several others you won't want to make either. On the way to creating and installing an awesome landscape, an informed design strategy will serve you well. This book will help. The specific knowledge presented in these pages will not only give you more ideas and options, it will give you more power in the landscape design and construction process.

Myth #1 *Anyone with a shovel and a pickup truck can landscape.*

To create and install a striking landscape, you need more than the right tools and the right spirit. The

Oregon Landscape Contractors' Board statistics show that more than three out of every five landscape businesses fail in the first five years. If so many landscape businesses are having such a tough time, maybe there's more to landscaping than meets the eye. Of all the landscape design and coaching sessions Fred's done, as well as the different sites and places we've both visited, one major problem rises to the top of the list: lack of planning.

Myth #2 *Landscaping is generic.*

Just as lifestyles have changed several times here in Bend since the sixties, so have the landscapes. They've gone from extremely minimal landscapes back then to the often high-tech and artistic landscapes of today. In between we had the juniper-shrubs-surrounding-the-lawn style. Then we had the generic sprinkler, sod and token planting area types. In the mid-eighties with Bend's "great recession," property changed hands and new styles started emerging again, ultimately upgrading to use more rock, berms and natural landscaping. In the nineties, more people brought more demand for livable backyards. In these sanctuaries, water features, lighting, pavers and even fire pits became much more common. Now in the new millennium with home prices high, landscapes have become an important part of any resale formula. It's ironic that house styles here haven't changed nearly as much as local landscaping styles.

Fashion and styles shift, so landscape design adjusts. Cars go through similar fads. Now, for example, mileage has become important again. Just yesteryear when SUVs were hot, it was all about the Hummer.

Countless projects get started without considering options or ultimate outcomes because many people believe one size fits all when it comes to landscaping. It doesn't. Building a landscape isn't like buying a car or a TV. Generic can work if all things are equal, but every site, every person and most buildings aren't equal. A successful design strategy requires customizing by an experienced professional. You wouldn't try to build your own house, car or TV. Thinking that you can build a landscape without some education and coaching is a money trap. So why take on a landscape alone?

Myth #3 *Landscapes and gardens are subjective.*

Judging from past invoices, 90 percent of Fred's clients needed someone to finish or fix their existing landscape. He sees and fixes many projects not done right the first time. Ask an appraiser or a realtor if these kinds of half-done projects crying out to be fixed detract from the selling price, and you'll hear the same response. If the entry is ugly, home buyers won't go in. That alone affects price. There's nothing subjective about appraised value. And there's nothing subjective about a landscape that needs work.

Landscapes that need work can get pretty ugly. We haven't seen it all," but we're probably getting close. Fred recently removed two sets of rock steps dangerously built one on top of the other, before finally locating new steps someplace else. He's had to re-grade (excavate) over irrigation installed too soon in the landscape process, remove ill-planned berms and rip out an overly ambitious irrigation system that had been installed before the landscape had been mapped out. A few times, he's advised clients not to take on projects with a low reward-to-cost ratio. The people who insisted on going ahead anyway wasted time and money. Unnecessary cost to the owners in all these cases: thousands.

Some people do landscape as therapy; we admit that we fall into this category as well. If this "therapy" doesn't include a vision or a plan, however, that's a problem. Add up the required materials and labor for the inevitable correction that will be required, and you're looking at an expensive "treatment" for you and your landscape.

The truth is most landscapes fail in part or in total, and need some kind of help. Most contractors don't know the secrets to fixing them, and even if they did they wouldn't tell their customers. This book is written to shift the odds in your favor. It's a map of sorts to help you navigate Central Oregon landscapes. We guarantee it! If after reading through this book and filling out the questionnaires, you aren't able to save time and money on your next project, return the book directly to us at Bend Pine Nursery for a full refund.

Secret #1 *Take an 80/20 problem-solving approach.*

Stay focused on what's most important (roughly 20 percent of your project list). By acknowledging problems and prioritizing them, you'll have time to plan and solve the big ones during your project. Don't get lost in all the imperfections and the "what ifs." There will always be more than enough to worry about! So save your mental energy for what's most important. Besides dealing with the bigger problems, you'll also need to have a vision and look for opportunities. Luckily, problems can actually create opportunities, something we'll explore in Chapter 3.

Good decisions made early on mean results will be maximized. The five most important steps to take simply involve recognizing your key challenge, utilizing strengths, generating multiple options, planning, and most importantly picking a good team. These all fall in that vital 20 percent category.

It's been said that "a problem well-defined is a problem half solved." Ignorance isn't bliss! After years in this field, the traps and pitfalls have become more obvious to me. Pain is just around the corner for people who drink and drive. The same goes for those who fail to plan and oversimplify landscaping. Sooner or later, they will feel the pain of wasted money and needless frustration.

Tip *Quick fixes usually lead to more problems.*

Understanding what makes landscapes work will help you seize opportunities and create value, because if you can't define success, how will you know whether you've achieved it? Fortunately, you don't need to reinvent the wheel to create beautiful landscapes. But you do need to make sure that you're doing it right.

Myth-busting helps you limit mistakes. By debunking false beliefs, it becomes obvious that results flow from our beliefs and knowledge. So the better you understand landscaping processes and choices, the better your project will turn out.

Tip *Responding to the unique features of your site is a proven method to create value in your landscape. Knowing your own needs and expectations is another.*

If done right, a landscape will make you money. A great landscape will also inspire you and make you feel alive. By considering your family and friends, you can all enjoy your place's livability. Why tackle a big landscape project? Because doing your landscape right can make your life that much better!

Chapter 2

Central Oregon's Challenges & Perks

Central Oregon has unique landscaping challenges. It can freeze any day of the year. The dry climate limits plant and tree selection. Vegetable gardens and some fruit trees grow here, but harvesting is a roll of the dice, since the growing season is so short. When Fred came to Bend in 1968 with his folks, his mom wanted to have a vegetable garden. After several disappointing seasons due to either early freezes or our beautiful and voracious local deer, she scaled back her attempts. Then there's the land. With Bend's population topping 75,000, most of the easy building sites are gone. What's left is mostly either built on already or rocky.

Myth #4 *We have topsoil here!*

Plan on dealing with rock and non-organic soil. Just because wet dirt looks dark doesn't mean it's rich in organics. Other than minerals from sand and volcanic dust, you won't find organic matter in the soil here that promotes plant growth.

Central Oregon faces the problems inherent with over-development. Rough building sites can spawn weed seeds that blow over onto neighboring properties, creating maintenance problems. Tighter and tighter lot sizes leave little room to landscape artfully.

The natural look and feel that attracted so many of us here in the first place is rapidly disappearing. The good news is that 90 percent of what's already been built locally can benefit from landscape remodeling or additions.

Tip *A fair number of contractors have more skill at selling than at doing a good job on your project, and the best contractors are in high demand, so choose wisely.*

One of the biggest challenges for someone just moving here is to adapt to this environment, because landscaping styles that worked in Seattle, Portland or San Francisco don't work well here. A recent tour of a nursery in the valley revealed that less than half of those plants would thrive in Bend. Boxwood and spirea shrubs do well here, as do pines and vine maples. Even some things that work in this area—like firs, sequoia and oaks—don't grow as lush or as thick as they do in wetter climates, and so tend to look anemic. They also die more easily. If you tour gardens in Portland or San Francisco, you will find more choices, but the majority won't hold up to our dry and cold climate.

Though plant selection is limited in Central Oregon, that's good in terms of maintenance. Because of the hard freezes and dry summers, we get a lot fewer weeds than wetter, warmer climates do.

Myth #5 *Deer won't eat it!*

Most people we talk with like the idea of low maintenance yards. Central Oregon is really made for these kinds of landscapes. Rocks and rockeries require zero upkeep; hardy trees and native grasses don't need much care either. And local deer, rabbits, squirrels, raccoons and other animals tend to feed themselves! As long as you protect your plants appropriately, you won't have to worry about them treating your yard as a salad bar.

Introducing trees like aspen or shrubs or rock daphne means adding watering systems. The good news is that by targeting your desired plants and trees with water, you promote what you like, while un-watered areas in your garden remain dry and easier to maintain.

Every eco-system has assets and liabilities. Bend is no exception. Because of our low humidity and cold temperatures, plant diseases and pests are minimal here. Compared to wetter or hotter climates, Central Oregon is an easy living place. Our sunny and usually dry weather means that enjoyment of the landscape during the season is pretty much a sure thing. That long, dry summer also provides us with a good-sized window for transforming our landscapes.

Landscaping is different from building construction in that you can't live in a half-finished house, but you can live with a partly done landscape. That can work to your advantage and your disadvantage.

Sometimes it's necessary because of time or budget constraints to build your landscape in phases that can extend even over a couple of years. You might want to focus first on creating an inviting entry or to seed excavated areas to control weed problems. Before you start, make sure the grading has been finished and done right. Once construction commences, any delays will cost you extra. So you need to be ready to see your undertaking through to completion from the beginning. An expensive or complicated project can require more planning and design time, so you may want to wait until you have a solid plan of action, even if that means missing this year's window. But by the time the next growing season rolls around, you will have a clear plan, contractor(s) and supplies lined up and be ready to go for it.

Beware of landscapes that have been slapped together to dress up a house and provide short-lived curb appeal. Some builders and developers probably think of landscaping as "putting lip stick on a pig." It's a way to sell houses faster and for more than they would get without dressing them up. Most lawns, for example, are just thrown down without good grading or supplements. Another tactic is to throw in some green trees and shrubs without adding an automatic irrigation system. It's a quick, cheap way to create visual impact, but too often the trees and shrubs that look good early during the spring just dry out and die during the hot and dry summers.

"Solutions," like laying sod over an area just to keep the dust down, usually create slippery slope problems later. Whether the landscaper neglected to grade or put down compost under the sod, these omissions show up later in the rest of the landscape. Sometimes the irrigation doesn't get put in. So the sod dries up and needs to be taken out, and then you're back at square one.

The problems inherent in these low quality landscapes aren't obvious at first, only showing up once you live with them a while. Landscape backtracking—called in the trade "landscape remodeling"—is usually required to upgrade the mix of poor layout, cheap parts and low-grade materials.

Even the best of home builders' landscapes almost always lack any real theme or usefulness. Besides just wanting to sell their spec homes and move on, builders live by straight lines and 90 degree angles. That's key when building a house. But landscapes aren't symmetrical and straight lines outside don't fit into the natural lines of trees, grasses, clouds, and rock. Landscapes are dynamic and always changing. The seasons, plant growth and death, and neighborhood development happen all around and all the time, while the house stays fixed in place. The best landscapes are done by someone who thinks in nature's terms and patterns.

Tip *Landscape construction needs to account for the changing landscape!*

I doubt that your dream is to have a generic tract home landscape. You want something special. Generic landscapes happen here as in so many other cities because they are fast and cheap. Unfortunately, simply starting a landscape where the spec builder left off is inferior to a taking holistic approach. Creating a quality landscape requires a response to the place itself, as well as to the owner's needs and desires.

Secret #2 *Recognize value. Seize opportunities.*

A landscape architect or designer takes in information you've gathered about the site, talks with you about your needs, and makes a personal visit to your property to come up with a drawing. Whether or not you hire a pro, however, keep in mind that nobody designs by themselves. It's a collaborative effort, one that works best if you can separate discussions about problems and concerns from those about inspiration and vision. Make no mistake, you'll need both mindsets to arrive at a successful result. But it's hard to think negatively and positively at the same time. Human brains short out like an electric circuit if you mix the two. The vision process requires a different mindset than critical problem-solving does.

To put it another way, you've probably heard the terms "don't rain on my parade" and "dreamer." To design and install a great landscape you'll need both expansive and critical minds, but not at the same time! Make a separate time to be intuitive and expansive in exploring and identifying opportunities. In the best of all possible worlds, brainstorm as many ideas and options with your team as you can. Once you've exhausted your creativity and all the ideas are down on paper, set a different time to scrutinize, judge and cull through the various options and ideas.

The personalities of your landscaping team members are more of a factor than you might imagine in this process. One person may get so excited about adding a water feature, he or she will forget to check the ground to see how rocky it is. With rock hammers renting for about $250 an hour, this can blow a project's budget sky high, especially since rock hammers don't cut through rock that quickly. Another person may be stuck on the status quo and resist change for the better by focusing on minor problems. So find a balance within your team, because ultimately your landscape results will reflect mindset.

You'll also want to invest in the value of your landscape by improving its livability and longevity. Since Bend's weather makes this a tough growing environment, find what thrives here.

Tip *Look around and see what's working in other landscapes.*

Despite plant selection limitations, Central Oregon offers many landscaping options. Water features can be beautiful and, with the right systems in place, can run all year long. Natural landscapes can blend in and accentuate the indigenous eco-system. Native grasses, hardy trees, shrubs and rock arrangements are readily available and a snap to care for. Though sod and irrigated landscapes are over-used as fallbacks, they provide kids and pets with room to run and a clean space to play. Using grass seed blends if some areas are shaded and some are full sun gives you healthy lawn in both places.

Explore your options. With homes being built right up next to each other, tree hedges can be a great improvement over fencing. They cost less money and they grow and fill in instead of ageing and getting knocked over. Tree hedges blend with the landscape and the surrounding natural features. They are more flexible and can be planted to hide specific views, e.g. neighbors' windows and doors. Birds like 'em too.

You want your landscape to "accentuate the positive and eliminate the negative." If all you have for a scenic view is the sky, capitalize on that. If you don't have a view of the river, build a water feature that you can enjoy outside and see from inside your house as well. Mountain views give you a reminder that we live in the High Cascades; build a berm in the foreground to visually connect the view of the background even more. If you don't have a good mountain view, a berm with boulders is a pleasing alternative. A few years back, Fred built a ten-foot berm with boulders, the largest weighing in at twelve tons. The owner of the house, located on the corner of Congress and St. Helens, called his new installation Mt. Gabor (naming it after himself, of course). Remember, you are part of your landscape, so give yourself room to be in it.

Some people want a more formal symmetrical garden. Why not? Others want an asymmetrical Chinese- or Japanese-style gardens. Much is possible here within our limits of climate and geography. Unfortunately, Central Oregon lacks state–of-the-art landscape design and botanical gardens. To get ideas, you'll either have to travel or scour magazines and books. Either way, stay flexible and realize that you're looking for inspiration more than for a blueprint. Keep in mind that you can also gain tremendous insight by evaluating those landscapes you don't like to see what doesn't work.

In addition, scour the local area for landscapes that have proven they can stand the test of time and still look great today. Don't get seduced into landscapes that look okay now simply because they have lots of fresh bark chips and new green sod. Some landscapes that look good now will deteriorate over time. Others that look alright now will thicken and flourish because they include the right kinds of trees and plants that were properly planted.

Finally, like the carpenter who measures twice before he cuts once, take the time to appraise your landscape fully. Identify what is wrong and what is good about your situation. Then focus your energy on smart design to make the most of what your site has to offer.

In the final analysis, your landscape problems are significant only because they give you the chance to respond and by doing so create something better. Design is what makes the difference. And the good news is that you are the designer.

Chapter 3

Design Is Discovery

As the designer, your first two tasks are to determine what you have to work with and how you want to use your space. That means not only analyzing your site's features, but also diagnosing its problems and possibilities.

Every site has its challenges and opportunities. Nowhere is this more true than in Central Oregon. It's your job to identify and then manage both effectively. By starting with a problem-solver mindset, you will find yourself way ahead of the curve. Having a heads-up on problems lurking in the project—and prioritizing them—reduces wasted money and time. When you identify an opportunity, you'll use a problem-solving mindset to implement the idea. By using most of your energy on the few most important parts of your project, you will maximize your resources.

Secret #3 *Discover what you're working with.*

Albert Einstein once said, "If I had twenty days to solve a problem I'd spend nineteen days defining it." Your first step is to pinpoint your site's problems and possibilities. To fix a leaking pipe first you must find the leak. You'll have to shut off the water main, then dig a hole below the leak deep enough to expose the broken pipes or fittings. Once you find the break, you'll need to measure the plumbing so you can get replacement parts. That's discovery. On a crime scene, the forensic team studies every little detail. That's also discovery. Doing your landscape homework involves the same meticulous research. You may not need to hire a home inspector, but you really should inspect your site yourself. Even after starting a landscape project, you'll discover the unexpected, but finding it sooner rather than later helps.

Design is all about discovery. In order to get a landscape that works for you and for your site, you have to figure out your site's attributes and challenges. Decide what you want and how you're going to use your space, and then apply proven landscape principles to this Central Oregon region. Three factors—place, people, and landscaping wisdom—will rise above all others as you do your designing.

Places have a natural mind and voice of their own. Interpreting that, however, can be like learning another language. Designing with nature is easier said than done. Do it anyway; it's rewarding and very satisfying to tune in to and be harmonious with nature. Go outside during different times of the day and night. Notice how the light plays on the place. Plan your landscape to align with your site's natural features. If you have a beautiful lava rock outcropping, play your design off that and use it as a focal point.

Just as each lot has its own personality, it also has its own shortcomings. You must have a big picture design perspective, while simultaneously paying attention to the details.

Tip *Hours spent simply looking at—and just walking around—your site as you plan can be some of your most productive design time.*

Do the exploration first. Before you put in a $25,000 landscape, make sure you'll be able to appreciate it from the curb as well as from inside the house. Consider your neighbors, the views (good and bad), seasonal changes, what areas get hot, what areas stay cold, etc. Some things are obvious, while recognizing others will require a little more observation. Looking isn't the same as seeing. If you've lived in your home a full year through the seasons, use the information you've acquired during that time to recognize and address problem areas, favorite views and hangouts, and other opportunities.

This kind of preparation is guaranteed to pay off. Design, however, is not open-ended. Some landscape ideas just won't fly no matter what. Not long ago, we saw a site where the house's utility lines (sewer, power, water) ran through the bottom of a pond under construction in the front yard. This kind of thing is just plain reckless. Recognize the difference between creative and crazy.

While planning your landscape, you have to look at the whole thing rather than the individual parts. No matter how much you love trees, it they're directly in front of windows blocking important views, they need to go or be pruned. They can also be a fire hazard, and safety always trumps art. A steep hillside can be the perfect place for a terraced rockery, but if it's out of sight from the house and hard to get to with equipment, maybe it's a project best left undone.

Once you have taken stock of your landscape problem, you'll want to focus on solutions. This is where you generate options for the best response called for by the circumstances. The cost of ignorance of the problem at hand is financial pain and time wasted on learning by trial and error. Spending time and money on landscape work and getting nothing in return is at best an exercise in frustration!

Unfortunately, plenty of people—from homeowners to developers—waste their money on dumb mistakes. They roll out sod over an old cinder roadbed and expect the lawn to thrive there. They commonly spend effort and money putting in plants that don't fit our climate and that die during the first freeze (which could easily be in July). These kinds of details simply must be considered, but that's not all it takes. To this day, after countless projects, we still need to visit and examine a site more than once before beginning to landscape. Even after starting a project, we will notice other important elements that apply to the overall design.

One of the biggest reasons to do good design is to circumvent problems before they happen. Problems only get resolved by recognizing them first. This is why copycat landscapes never turn out as expected.

Tip *Trying to do the exact same design that you like someplace else is often misguided because your landscape isn't someplace else.*

The variables and differences between sites, owners, houses, and neighboring features don't get responded to when you're trying to totally copy a design. Taking pieces of a successful design—especially a local one—can work great, as long as you integrate those ideas with your setting.

Sites differ around Central Oregon; we even have different micro-climates. Along the river it's a bit more protected and humid. To the South, more snow falls and the growing season is shorter. West toward the mountains is wetter. East of town, you'll find a dryer, more arid eco-system. There are sites as small as a tenth of an acre while others have several acres. On the small sites after the building, driveway and sidewalks go in, not much is left to landscape. On bigger properties there are just too many square feet to try to landscape the whole place. A few areas have clay. Some areas have ground water very close to the surface; others have hard pan barely covered by soil. Rock is generally everywhere, but the amounts and types vary.

Tip *By trying to copy another landscape, you are forgetting to solve and respond to the problems unique to you and your place.*

This can't be repeated enough. Landscapes are simply not a one size fits all proposition. For starters, each building on a site has its own footprint, elevations, grade, parking, etc. The views, solar exposure, and surrounding context need to be considered. Besides, every owner has differing ideas, needs and expectations.

Generic landscapes are even less creative, and unfortunately some of our most common. Built for expediency, tract home landscapes go to the lowest bidder. These low-end jobs cut corners and oversimplify to the point of being very boring. Usually they try to cover as much dirt as possible with sod lawns, and then dot a few areas with cheap plants. You'll often see a whole row of front yards done in the exact same way.

Generic landscapes are usually cheap and can be done quickly without much preparation. But because they don't reflect the owners' needs, the site characteristics or the resale value, this kind of landscape is the most likely to need remodeling. Unfortunately, attempts to remodel these landscapes often don't work because new problems just get put on top of old problems. The contrast between old and new doesn't usually fit and so more time and money is wasted even as the owners try to limit spending.

I know for a fact that poor design leads to poor results. We've learned this the hard way ourselves. So take a little time and don't be in a rush to do something until you fully understand the situation.

Tip *Preparation creates knowledge and knowledge improves results.*

Your first design step is discovering what's there—and what really matters—so you can use that knowledge to your advantage. You might have a big pile of excavated rock on-site. Become a design alchemist—where and how can these rocks (or other resource) be utilized? Retaining walls or rockeries add value to a property, so if you have it, use it. Limitations of size or strange lot lines can be turned around to an advantage if you are thoughtful about the design.

The Chinese have a symbol that means both crisis and opportunity. If you have to take out an old outdated and ugly landscape, perhaps you can transplant many or all of the trees and shrubs. Sometimes terrible landscapes are good because you can just tear the whole thing out and start totally fresh.

So part of design involves figuring out how to make the most of what you have and how much you have to do and spend. An entry with little room to landscape can be done up with a high-impact treatment that provides an absolute "wow" factor. Yet since the space is small, the head-turning treatment won't eat into too much of the overall budget. A side yard can be graveled for utility purposes instead of being given a full-out landscape, and the savings can be applied to the living and prominent areas instead.

Using pictures to provide design ideas can be helpful. However, mistaking the map for the territory is a major mistake. The climate, the feel of the place, the various points of view, existing plants and trees, etc., won't translate to a two-dimensional drawing or photo.

Videos capture the essence of a place even less well. Landscapes aren't flat, they are dimensional and set in a context that simply won't show up in a flat picture or screen. There's just no way to encapsulate the whole look of a place on film. When Fred designed the landscape for the 1995 ABC miniseries "McKenna," he had to create a complete landscape that would blend the settings together. Yet the TV series never captured the scope of the whole $250,000 landscape project on screen.

We have bid countless projects where partially thought out plans only confused the design. It's not that uncommon to have a drawing show South where North should be or neglects to display the site's major features.

Recently we went to bid on a small project that the clients had spent $1,000 getting drawn up. The owners had successfully used a plan by that same designer in San Francisco, and the plan looked good on paper. Instead of visiting the site in Bend, however, the designer had used a couple of photos of the house to get "her bearings." As a result, the garden she designed was more visible from the road than from the house. In addition, her site plan failed to account for the huge rock outcroppings covering half the site. Finally, though the plan was fairly well researched plant-wise in terms of what would work in our climate, her plant choices didn't match what local nurseries carry. Trying to install this design as shown would have cost four times as much as necessary, not looked anywhere near as good as the ultimate landscape, and wouldn't have been seen from the home's interior.

Design ultimately needs to be an inspired response to a problem and a creative solution. Just the act of discovering the key problems and challenges gets you nearer to a solution. Clients of ours had a bad deer problem. They liked having deer around, but didn't like how the deer decimated their plants. The solution came from responding to the second-story view of the mountains. On the ground level we used rock, mulch, and extremely hardy and tough deer-resistant plantings, rockeries and wood art. New planters and even a small water feature on the upper deck allowed our clients to enjoy the outdoors while keeping their new landscape away from the hungry deer. On both levels, this creative and effective response solved the problem they faced.

Clearly, landscape challenges can actually point the way to wonderfully effective designs. A car dealership client (Robberson Ford) had a seasonal problem when the snow came and was sanded with red cinders. Both the snow and red cinders got plowed up onto the car lot in piles. By designing planter beds with big red boulders, the colors and shapes matched up during the wintertime. Then in the spring, annuals were added to existing trees and perennial flowers to dress up the property for the warm season. With this design, the dealership looks good all year-round.

In both these examples, regard for the site and the circumstances set the stage for good design. Without discovering what's happening on-site before drawing up plans, neither the cinder-filled snow nor the hungry deer problem would have been accommodated.

Once you've identified your site's attributes and drawbacks, you need to consider yourself, what you're looking for and how you want to use the site. Some people want a formal look; some want high-touch and livability. Others want to look out the kitchen window and see a water feature. Still others want to host gatherings and parties in their landscapes, or even do business there.

Tip *The price you pay for a car is similar to what a landscape will cost you.*

Your purpose will largely determine the scope of the project. A home builder or developer has the challenge to sell his or her property, whereas a homeowner wants livability and something to be proud of. A car just to commute to work can be a low-priced model. Likewise, the landscape a builder puts in just needs to get the prospective buyers to come inside and hopefully make an offer. A family car for vacations, holidays and summers needs to be a car built for comfort, and one you can take pride in. Similarly, a landscape that is going to get used needs livability features as well as visual impact.

Budget is always part of the design equation. If you're the type who wants only the best of everything, high-end landscapes can deliver high performance and as many bells and whistles as you'd like. Still, between us, we've done dozens of commercial and industrial landscapes, hundreds of homeowner landscapes, and a landscape for ABC, and not a single one of those clients had an unlimited budget.

Nowhere is the old adage "penny wise, pound foolish" more appropriate than at this stage of your landscaping project. As the mechanic in an old TV ad used to say, you can pay me now for an oil filter (prevention) or pay me later for a new engine (cure). Take the time to discover your best design options, or assume that you'll be paying to fix your landscape or selling your property for significantly less that it would otherwise be worth down the line. You don't need to reinvent the wheel. The school of hard knocks is for knuckleheads. We should know, we've still got a few lumps of our own to prove it!

Design should be interesting and fun, but it's not an end in itself. Enjoy it and take the time required of the process, but remember your objective is to create a usable landscape. Be a problem-solver without being overly critical; you're not sending a rocket to the moon or doing heart surgery here. Have *fun* with it. Discover what's there first. Look for opportunities. Take advantage of the resources on-site and the resources of your team. Remember the design you develop is your response to a problem and a creative challenge. It should include both self-expression and self-discipline. With this kind of mindset you'll be on your way to creating a great landscape outcome.

Chapter 4

Making a Plan

Now that you have identified what you have to work with, what you are up against, and what the area demands, you need to plan out your space. The secret is knowing how to value the key areas and prioritize the work accordingly.

As we've mentioned, this can best be done by using an 80/20 approach. That means focusing on the most important 20 percent of your lot's square footage—the cream of the crop or the best slice of the pie. That's where you'll get the best bang for your buck. This mindset will keep you focused on the payoff areas throughout the process. It will steer you away from wasting efforts and dollars on trivial matters that can slow your project's progress.

As we saw in the last chapter, part of 80/20 involves identifying major problems so you can fix them. Without recognizing a problem first, you can't get to a solution. What's missing or needs fixing? Drainage, ugly views, or access can be problems that call out to be resolved.

After admitting and even embracing your problems (Secret #1), shift and explore possible opportunities (Secret #2). Tag those assets that already exist and can be put to good use, including a pile of boulders, a pile of good dirt, plants that can be recycled or a stunning view on which you can capitalize.

Most important, prioritize. Wherever you look, notice and seek value. Don't waste money, but don't be cheap either. Focus your attention and resources on what's most important. And don't forget to make the most of the one thing that every house shares: the entry.

Secret #4 *Invest in a great entry.*

An entry is like packaging—it grabs attention in a positive way and invites use. Great first impressions and curb appeal make all the difference. Entries are also a trademark for both you and your place. Since they represent you to guests, you want to dress up your entry for success. Ultimately your entry will sell you or your house well or poorly! Finally, entries need to be safe and easy to navigate while walking, not just because people coming to your front door could fall, but because in our litigious society they could then sue you as well.

Tip *Your entry, which extends from the public street or road to your front door, sells you and your house.*

In short, giving serious consideration to the space from street to front door is good design. Entries usually are smaller in square footage, but high in impact. A dreary, unkempt, uninteresting entry has a strong negative impact on people. Cramped sidewalks, cheap steps or stairs, and incomplete landscaping at the entry—because the area is such a focal point—are more obvious than they would be elsewhere. So the first step (no pun intended) is to clean up and complete unsightly aspects of your entry. The good news is entries don't take up much space, so you can splurge on specimen plants and trees that really attract people's attention as they drive up and walk into your home. They can also provide you with an alternative sitting area that's either warmer or cooler than the other side of the house.

Secret #5 *Build outdoor rooms.*

Here's another little-appreciated 80/20 fact: Outdoor rooms add livability to your landscape and value to your home by extending its usable space. Outdoor rooms are part of your home's overall footprint, and compared to interior space are remarkably inexpensive. You should capitalize on this bargain.

Tip *The price per square foot for outside living space is usually less than 5 percent of interior space.*

Clearly, utilizing this outside space well is a wise investment. But sometimes in the pursuit of style or mimicking what the neighbors are doing, we lose perspective. Reality check! Just as sprinklers serve plants' needs for water, landscapes should serve people's needs for use and enjoyment. So you want to intentionally create spaces for activities, like sitting, eating, storage, kids' play, privacy, hobbies, parties and more. Maximize the value of your landscape's livability and lifestyle possibilities by evaluating the wants and needs of yourself, your family and your friends.

What you decide to do depends on how much room you have and on your priorities. The rooms inside of your home serve functions vis-à-vis living—you sleep in some, cook, entertain, watch TV or read in others. Outdoor rooms ought to serve functions too. You'll need to consider hardscaped, native and planted areas when deciding on how much to have of each in your final landscape. Why not enjoy mini vacations in your own well-planned and installed back yard? You can eat and entertain in your outdoor dining area. You can create awesome rooms for family gatherings and parties, or build an outdoor shower next to your hot tub.

Consider how you want to live in your outdoor space and plan accordingly. Options include hammocks or sofas for sleeping, benches or square rocks for sitting, kids' rooms for playing games, campsites for out-of-towners, places to BBQ, boulder fire pits to sit around or compost piles for recycling and gardening.

You can invite nature into your home. Nature lovers will want to consider waterfalls and re-naturalized areas, since they attract wildlife. The right plants, like fragrant Butterfly Bushes, will also attract animals, birds and, yes, butterflies. Maybe you'd like a garden sanctuary that provides a space for topiary hedges, a water feature, and/or a sculpture. It's your call. By customizing your landscape space, you can extend your living space while connecting with nature for an elegant—or even downright rustic—outdoor experience.

My ceramics teacher taught us that it's not the fired and glazed clay that is most important, it's really the usable space the clay provides. A cup has to hold liquid to be a cup. A home is lived in all year round, with holidays, special occasions (birthdays, weddings, anniversaries, etc.), pot lucks and BBQs. By considering how long you will live at this address, you can start looking at the design with a time frame—and lifestyle—in mind. That's what will make your outdoor space livable.

Once you've identified your outdoor rooms, you want to integrate those into the natural context so they come together as a whole. Unity is all too often neglected. Unity is like a fresh deep blanket of snow that covers everything from plants to hardscape to fences and more. The hard lines that separate one area from the next are erased. It's all one piece, with no rough or sharp edges, no boundaries.

Wholeness and completion of a theme are inherent in a unified landscape. The opposite of unity is an eclectic, piecemeal hodgepodge of different unfinished vignettes. The clutter such a place creates is uncomfortable to be around and to look at. Conversely, a place that connects well to its surrounding is harmonious and relaxing.

Secret #6 *Unify—create a sense of place.*

To achieve unity in your landscape, fit your landscape into the surrounding context. Work within the elements, lines and patterns of the encompassing area.

Even simply following the grade lines of your site and incorporating native plants will help enhance unity. Lawns can connect landscapes, but they need to fit into the bigger framework of the neighborhood, as well as the natural land and flora.

Unity looks simple because it eliminates unnecessary distracting clutter. To innovate, you must first eliminate; some would say to create you must destroy. By eliminating the funk and junk, you make room for something better. Be like a maid or seamstress for your landscape's clean-up and construction. Don't be afraid to be a bit ruthless. Sometimes something good can get in the way of something that could be great.

You also want to pay attention to a variety of design theories and ideas like Feng Shui, the Chinese art of placement or Vaastu Shastra, the Indian version. These can help you see nature's flowing energy when designing your landscape. Study botanical gardens when you travel. Notice how the gardens interface with their surroundings.

Though keeping things simple probably represents 80 percent of unity, connections and spirit also play roles. A place that reflects these three components will exude elegance and charm. If you can find the essence of landscaping that fits both the person and the place, that's unity, too.

You are a resource and an asset, so fit yourself into the formula. Your landscape should be an expression of you and your nature. Just as your car, clothes, and books speak for you, what do you want your landscape to say about you?

How do you see yourself living with your landscape? Design your hobbies and skills into your landscape project. How will your family and friends fit in? In addition to socializing together in—or overlooking—your landscape once it's completed, you may be able to put them to work during its construction. Their skill sets or lifestyles may impact your design decisions.

So will your personal preferences. What kind of management of the landscape are you likely to pursue? Will you mow your own lawn or hire it out? Everyone likes low maintenance, but some want a garden to work in, while others only want to look out a window to see their beautiful yard.

Creating a dynamic landscape you can be proud of requires a good overview of the process before you start. Respond to your lot, use elements that work locally, and incorporate yourself into the picture. You benefit from the substantial value returned on your investment when you use an 80/20 decision mindset.

Cost is always a factor, but don't forget your goal—you want impact from your investment. Silver may be cheaper than gold, but gold is much more valued. When the whole is greater than the sum of the parts, value is maximized.

In the next chapter we'll go through your choices of elements and the implementation steps that add up to a complete landscape. For specifics on plant selection and more local issues and ideas read on to Chapter 6. When you are ready to participate a little more actively in the process, use the final chapter to get yourself moving farther along the curve toward creating your own outstanding landscape.

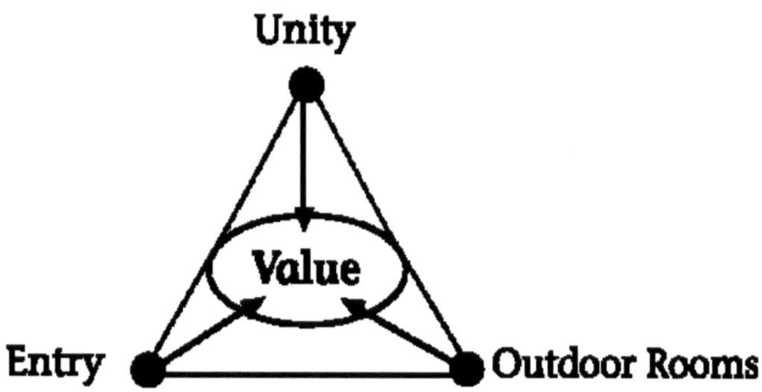

Creating Value

Chapter 5

Putting the Elements in Place

Once you have a design, you need a plan of action. Whether you're going to do some—or all—of the work yourself, you need to know the basics of what it takes to build your landscape. The sequence of projects and events, the mix of materials, and inventory management all need consideration. Timing and orchestrating the work will smooth— or stall—your project's progress. And as we all know, time is money. So you want to come equipped with knowledge to get the job done right from the outset.

Physically-oriented work requires help. Before you take on a heavy load of work for yourself consider the nature of the beast. You'll be working outside and the weather and the seasons have their impacts. In addition, building berms, patios, or pathways, moving boulders for retaining walls, constructing waterfalls and ponds, and grading for lawns and other outdoor rooms is physically straining work. We've had clients take on too much of it themselves and hurt their bodies in the process.

Tip *Just because you can do something doesn't mean you should do it!*

Written plan, drawn plan or no plan, an elegant and simple landscape takes a lot of preparation and thinking. A design that only uses one or two systems—e.g. sod and sprinklers, or pavers and boulders—can be called landscape work, but it is not complete. As we saw in the last chapter, a great landscape is able to balance several elements. That means that you or your general contractor will need to coordinate several different building systems. Otherwise the end of the project keeps getting pushed out, costing more money and creating unneeded frustration. Many landscapes don't ever get finished. Don't let this happen to you. Be honest and open about what it will really take to complete your landscape the first time around.

Be careful of contractors who bid only part of your project, leaving too much to do later and too little budget to do it with. Remember that salesmanship doesn't necessarily include workmanship! I've fixed several landscapes where a landscaper "friend" did the job, but sadly, wasn't any good at it. Just because somebody wants your job doesn't make him or her qualified! Ponds, for example, can't be done right by just any excavating contractor. Just because a contractor can dig a hole doesn't mean he or she knows water features.

When choosing contractors, keep in mind that some landscapers only really do irrigation and lawns. They may be technically great at putting in sod and irrigation, but not so good at conceptualizing the big picture. Landscapers sometimes try to do too much of the work themselves. They bid out the parts of the job they aren't really good at, just to get all the work.

Higher-end work takes a team. After doing construction and landscape for thirty-five years, Fred still uses many specialist sub-contactors. One person alone is not enough to get the best landscaping results, which is why most pros don't do it all. Good concrete contractors don't install wooden decks, paver guys don't know boulders, etc.

It's *your* job to sort all this out.

Which gets us back to design and management. If you realize that your project involves several building systems like decking, patio, lawn, irrigation, a water feature, grading and boulders, plants, utilities and more, you may need a general contractor to manage the project. Alternatively, having someone serve as project superintendent will keep mix-ups to a minimum.

Whether or not you hire someone to oversee the project, somebody's going to have to hire the specialists. As the owner of the property, you usually hire deck, masonry, patio and concrete contractors yourself. A general contractor can hire the rest of the specialists (or indeed all of them if you prefer), since they usually already have a network to call. If you're doing the hiring, remember that lighting should be done by someone with training and experience—either a landscape lighting specialist or an electrician. For specialties like berms, terracing, boulders and sculpted sites, Fred's company Sculptural Landscapes is well known throughout Central Oregon.

Tip *Don't hire a specialist for a manager and don't hire a generalist for features such as masonry, stamped concrete or other craftsman-level projects.*

The more building systems a project needs, the higher the project's cost. On the other hand, leaving out necessities may save money, but it won't improve the final landscape. And doing things wrong is simply a waste!

Who you buy from is just as important as who you hire. Buy from stores with specialists who can actually advise you about your purchase. The one-stop building centers don't employ experts … at least we have yet to meet one there. On the other hand, if you already know what parts or materials you really need, they *can* save you money in some situations.

Specialty stores have a wider selection in their niche of materials and tools and have more experienced staff, so you'll want to go to the right store for the right product. Decking materials, including weatherproof composite types, come from lumber yards or building centers (e.g. Backstrom's Builders or Miller Lumber). Concrete is sold and delivered by sand and gravel companies. Willamette Greystone has mega tons of pavers, bricks and block. Empire Stone is great for natural rock. Places in Bend like Searings or Horizon Professional Landscape Supply have irrigation and electrical supplies. Lawns need compost under them, bark mulch next to them and sod or seed over the compost. Check Instant Landscape for these supplies. Round Butte Seed is great for weed and pest control, as well as farm and garden supplies. Ponds, pools and spas require specialty suppliers and a bit of research.

Before you go shopping, you have to make decisions about what you need. We've already discussed taking a little time to examine preexisting systems—both natural and what the homeowner or builder left for you.

Some things you'll want to save. There may be native grasses already keeping some dust down, so don't disturb them during construction. You may have a semi-functional irrigation system. Existing plumbing may simply need to be cut back and capped off. If parts of the landscape aren't broken, why take them out and start over?

You'll want to remove other aspects of your landscape. If an ugly old deck won't last for a couple more years and has missing or broken boards, why keep it? Bumpy, dried out lawns may not be worth trying to resuscitate.

It's up to *you* to discriminate between what stays and what goes, as well as what you want to add into the equation.

The final permanent hardscape elements need to fit together like a jigsaw puzzle. Though you probably won't do your own utility hook-ups, knowing about them will help you ensure that you get what you need. Irrigation needs to evenly water lawns (with double coverage) and to target plant and tree roots. You'll need to run electric lines for pumps, lighting, outdoor kitchens or workshops, etc. Sometimes gas is required for BBQs, fire pits, or even tiki torches, which means that you'll need to have conduits and gas piping installed. Specialty plumbing for outdoor kitchens, spas and showers requires drainage and freeze protection.

Tip *Call for existing utility locates before you start construction; various utility companies will come out and mark the locations of your existing lines.*

Setting the stage as work progresses takes timing. While you won't want to install conduits so early that your contractor(s) loses track of them, you also don't want to wait too long to put them in and have to disturb areas already built.

Tip *Use a free site plan.*

Newer homes often come with building plans and a site plan. Part of the original construction package, site plans provide detailed information about your property on a bigger and better scale than the next two options. However, something is better than nothing. So if you haven't been provided with a set of the construction plans for your home, local title companies can print up a simple version of your house's plotted site that includes measurements. Alternatively, county or city sewer or septic locate maps include site measurements. Then if you need further plans drawn professionally, at least you already have a site plan started and have gathered relevant facts and detailed measurements about your site.

Tip *Mark the utility conduits as you put them in, so you can find them later.*

Whether or not you have a site plan, you'll need to mark your property lines and what's underground before construction starts. You can use little wire flags, wooden stakes, spray paint or even a garden hose to mark the layout for your utilities, lawn edges or water features.

If you're planning a big landscape project, an organization system will ensure that the information you need in the months to come is at your fingertips. Keep a project folder with lists of materials, vendors and plans. Include a file for receipts. You'll also want to track your landscape project's progress. Keep a list of what gets done as work progresses. That will help you make sure that nothing gets missed, and give you the information you need to gauge when progress payments are due.

Tip *Keep a simple list of contractors and supplier phone numbers handy.*

Okay. Now it's time to get physical. That starts with site clean-up, which includes removing trash, dead plants and junk rock. Next you'll want to stockpile and stage the materials you need to do the job.

Your next task is grading your site. Top-notch professional grading includes minimizing steps, grading for water features and fire pits, and creating level spaces without everything being boringly flat. Great grading brings vertical interest to your landscape. Berms with rock "outcroppings" provide planting areas. Building your water feature into a berm will naturally connect it to your overall theme.

Unfortunately, grading is typically underdone, resulting in more complicated and compromised grade issues—as well as more expensive construction down the line. It's easy even for professionals to make grading mistakes without using transits, levels or water. Once the grade starts to be compromised, code drainage, access, and extra work usually follow. Cosmetic hillsides without proper materials to hold back the bank, for example, will lead to a lot of shoring up in the future as your lovely hill turns into a not so lovely mess. The initial small investment made in site work lowers final—and future—project costs and looks so much better.

Tip *Your site's grade needs to provide a platform for the yard's activities and construction.*

When grading, drainage must be considered sooner or later. Sooner is better. Ground compaction may be necessary, since when you excavate and refill an area, that ground loses compaction. The site is brought to rough grade to make sure that any additions line up with the top of the final grade. Then, most hardscapes will require gravel or base material for support.

Tip *Most excavators usually do flat work and install utility mains for developments, but sometimes their services are needed for big rock and material logistics on landscapes.*

Once you've got your site rough-graded, it's time to install your irrigation system. Automatic irrigation takes 24-volt electric valves and a timer, requires a backflow device and gets hooked up to the water main.

It's important to be able to adjust water delivery for seasonal fluctuations and plant growth. Although some homeowners put in their own irrigation systems, these are much harder to do right than they look, and usually include pop-up sprinkler heads with various designs and capacities. Sprinklers with the right nozzle can water long thin sidewalk lawn medians. As we mentioned earlier, remember that no nozzle sprays uniformly, so always have double coverage over lawns to minimize watering gaps. Extra long pop-ups can water flower beds. Some heads can cover big distances. Drip systems can be used together with pop-ups or without them, but not in the same zone. Drip is the most water-conserving and the small tubing doesn't need to be buried as deeply. There are different emitters and even some micro heads for pots on decks, etc.

When pumping from a well, cistern or pond fed by an irrigation ditch, another level of plumbing is needed. Farm pump and irrigation vendors, like Thompson Pump & Irrigation, can help you with well water and non-pressurized water sources. The water system ought to be tailored to serve the water needs of the plants in your landscape. Irrigation with nothing to water would be pretty silly.

Getting your site materials right will minimize problems as the project develops. For example, good dirt isn't always a very stable foundation for a berm—a mix of small rock and cheap dirt will actually work better for a solid base and save you money.

It's a different story, however, when it comes to planting or to raking out dirt on which lawns will be installed. Topsoil in Central Oregon is razor thin at best, so supplementing your soil around plant roots is required. To build your landscape, you should add planting medium to all plants including sod lawns. Freshly-excavated sites are dust-makers in the summer and erosion problems waiting to happen in the winter. Mulching beds and reseeding excavated or disturbed areas is a simple and effective fix. If you are seeding for native grasses or flowers, adding compost makes sense.

The grasses that work here are cool-season varieties. They flourish in spring and fall, but need about three times more water during the hot summer months. By contrast, we have a super low maintenance lawn. For the hottest two months of the year, we deep water it no more than once a week. The trick is using drought tolerant fescue seed and supplementing with compost. The lawn may not be as lush as some, but we also only need to mow it once a year.

Tip *If you want to keep dust down use mulch, not compost (mulch retards grass or weed growth, compost promotes it).*

Basically, you want to work *with* nature rather than against it. Nature's system of having trees or forests for canopy and plants at ground level to help hold soil and water has worked for millennia. It's widely known that removing too many trees compromises the plants under their canopy and soon the soil. The result? Erosion and non-organic soil with little ability to hold water.

The elements will impact your outdoor spaces, too. The seasons bring challenges, and you'll need to manage their impact. Winter can mean broken pipes and limited access. Rainy downpours can cause serious erosion damage. Late summer hot days can dry out and kill plant and tree roots, while the dryness also means that dust gets blown around at the first bit of wind. Being prepared in advance for these conditions will save you huge repair bills and a lot of angst.

Knowing what you're up against, especially in Central Oregon, will make or break your landscape. A lawn, for example, takes grading, organics and the right seed choice. Maintaining your lawn will at the very least demand regular mowing, fertilizing and the correct water delivery. Lawns may also need periodic thatching or aeration to let the roots get what they need in terms of air and water. Nothing lasts forever, including lawns. Disease, compaction and age take their toll. Assuming that under-watering isn't the issue, less vigorous or dry spots on your lawn can be dealt with by mixing compost and seed, and then over-seeding the trouble spots.

Tip *The native grasses of our high desert ecosystem require little water and are thus drought tolerant.*

But we're getting ahead of ourselves. Before you worry about caring for your lawn, you'll need to make decisions about your hardscape options. These include masonry rock features, retaining walls, paver patios and walkways, concrete patios, steps, parking, pools or spas, and all the utilities that feed them. As we've said earlier, make sure that the utilities that serve the hardscapes and foundation materials are in place early in the process. Paver or concrete patios create flat, fire-proof, hard-to-hurt areas in your landscape. Make sure to provide drainage off these areas, including downspouts from your roof.

Tip *You'll also want to use gravel and sand as a base underneath paver patios.*

Your hardscape choices will dictate systems and materials. Building walls with block will keep hills from shifting, for example, but reinforcing first and then providing drainage for extreme rain conditions are a must. Building a wall with dry stacked rock, which is porous, requires different engineering than having a mason build a solid block wall on concrete footing and then mortar the decorative rock onto the block. Rock steps can be desirable but they can also be uneven and slick when wet, so watch out for safety issues.

Of course, your choices will also be dictated by a sense of aesthetics and your personal style. Again, the considerations are many. You may want stamped or colored concrete. Texturing concrete walls or planters has become increasingly common; downtown Bend has about twenty-four artistic textured concrete planters.

Once you've decided on the medium, you still have presentation options. For example, building your patio just off the deck and at the same level as the lawn makes a great transition. The patio can function as a level step into your landscape.

Water features can be your landscape's *pièce de resistance*, but the good ones are more complicated than they seem. The real pros at building water features go out in nature and study natural waterfalls. Positioning weirs (the way a special stone cuts or presents the water) and distributing water correctly is an art that creates a look of more water being pumped than actually is.

Multiple systems must also function together to make a water feature work. All too often, that doesn't happen. At least three out of four local water features don't work; most leak, grow algae or look bad. We've had to charge clients as much to fix their water features as they originally paid to buy and install them.

When planning for a water feature, first decide how large it will be. Remember that the pump required to move the water uses electricity, so consider your operating cost when making your purchase and design decisions. Next, figure out where you want to situate your water feature. Place the feature so you can see it from inside the house. The sound projects straight out from the water course and falls, so point it in the best direction to take advantage of the way sound carries.

Tip *Keep in mind that built in the right place and in the right way, a water feature can mask road noise.*

To ensure that you end up with a natural-looking water feature with clear running water, have the water filtered mechanically and biologically. A water course, aquatic plants, a skimmer and a biofalls filter will all contribute to that goal. You'll probably use a liner, but you should also use fabric to protect that liner. You need to make sure that power for the pump(s) and lighting is done to code. You'll also need a water source to keep the water feature full, as well as periodic maintenance. Figure out where you want to locate the light and operation off/on switches for easy access. You can run your water feature year-round with the right kind of plumbing and a small heater. That way the pond won't freeze over completely and burn up the pump, which is what happens when water can't reach it through the ice. If you're not going to run your water feature in the winter, drain it. Otherwise, it'll be a mess come spring.

Keep in mind that safety around a water feature is a legally required element; this issue is even getting more attention in Congress. Any water feature over two feet in depth must be covered when not in use, or the yard (or feature) must be fenced in.

If you want to be able to lounge in your water feature year-round, you'll want to think pool and spa. Remember, both pools and spas require chemicals and vigilant maintenance to avoid illness from pathogens.

Pools and ponds add luxury to your home and landscape, but, like water features, they need to be installed by an experienced (pool or pond) builder. Even a simple hot tub needs power, water, chemical maintenance, a cover and a concrete pad. Bigger pools, even if delivered to the site, require onsite construction excavation, plumbing and more. Permits and scheduling for pools can take more time, so getting started in the process sooner is important.

If your dream home needs a pool, I'll bet it'll cost you more than you originally thought. You need to know going in that money "sunk" into a pool won't be easy to recoup when you sell. If return on investment is your goal, ponds and water features may be safer bets (if built right). Pools serve best for enjoyment (I love them), but like buying a new car, they are not great investments.

Now that we've covered the building materials and contractors, your next step involves decisions about what plants will adorn your landscape. In Central Oregon, that's not as obvious as it might seem.

Problem Solving

PART 2

THE PLANTSCAPE

Chapter 6

Selecting Plants That Thrive in Bend

Once you have your landscape plan and have identified the features of your site and how you want to use the space, you can begin selecting the trees and plants that will best fulfill your needs for the landscape, climate and conditions.

Trees and plants serve many purposes in your landscape. They help to organize and shape the space of your landscape. They guide you visually and physically through the landscape—creating direction, pathways and outdoor rooms—and highlight points of interest. Trees and shrubs give shade and protection from sun, wind, and dust, and even absorb pollutants out of the air. They can screen out unwanted views, giving privacy. They also provide color, texture and beauty with flowers, foliage and needles. Trees and plants help to anchor the house to the land and create a transition or bridge from the house to the surrounding environment and neighborhood. They are living works of art with their shapes and colors, bringing joy, peace, comfort and beauty to the surroundings. However, they won't do any of that if they don't thrive.

The right selection of trees and plants can not only make or break your landscape, it can make or break your budget, especially in a region where frost is a possibility 365 days per year. Trees and plants are rated by the USDA (United States Department of Agriculture) for climatic conditions. The rating is indicated by zone, based on the minimum temperatures of each region throughout the country. Zones range from 1 being the most extreme cold temperatures to 10 being the mildest climate. Here in Central Oregon we are rated as Zone 5 with minimum temperatures ranging from -20 to -10 degrees Fahrenheit. However, certain areas in our region, especially those of higher elevations such as Sunriver and La Pine, often run colder. Sarah's rule of thumb is that trees or plants rated Zone 1 to 4 are usually a safe bet. However, due to global warming, zones are shifting and you may be able to grow plants that would normally fall in Zone 6 (a warmer climate). Using supplements (which we'll discuss later) can also expand the variety of plant choices.

Even those plants or trees that can technically survive, however, won't necessarily thrive. We had a client who wanted to grow bamboo. While she did find a variety that could endure the winter, the plant never grew. Each year the bamboo would make an effort, but when the cold weather set in it would die back almost to the ground. After a couple of years it was alive, but smaller than when she had planted it. It never really took off and certainly did not provide the privacy my client had anticipated.

Zone is not the only factor you need to consider. In order to choose the right plant for the right place and the right purpose in your landscape, you need to know whether your choice of tree or plant thrives in shade, sun, or part shade. If you put a shade-loving plant in full sun, chances are high that it will scorch and shrivel.

You also need to consider the growth habits of the trees and plants you choose. If you have a small space that needs filling, don't plant a tree that quickly grows very large, unless you want an immediate screen. Conversely, don't choose small trees that grow slowly if you're trying to hide the monstrosity next door. If you require that the tree not get too tall, there are many dwarf and semi-dwarf species of both broadleaf and evergreen trees and shrubs that work well here. Also consider whether you need screening twelve months a year or just in summer when you spend time outdoors. For year-round screening, you want an evergreen tree or shrub; for a summertime screen you can use a deciduous tree or shrub.

The sizes, shapes and textures that the trees and shrubs take on as they mature will also influence your decisions. While most evergreen trees are pyramidal in shape, others, like Arborvitae or columnar Scots pine, are more straight up and down. Some can turn into massive hedges, like all the juniper shrubs you see in older neighborhoods, if not vigorously pruned and maintained. Deciduous trees and shrubs have a wide variety of shapes and sizes. Usually the shape of these trees is reflected in the canopy of the leaves. Some are like big round balls, others more oval- or vase-shaped. Some are uniform and symmetrical, while others are more free-flowing and asymmetrical. The same is true with shrubs. You can find almost any shape you need for your landscape. If you have a narrow space, opt for a columnar tree or shrub.

The leaves or needles of the trees and shrubs provide texture and come in every shape and size imaginable: round, pointy, long, short, fat, skinny, etc. The different shape of the leaves and needles evoke different feelings. Some feel and appear soft, some hard, some formal, some more natural and informal. Experiment with shape, size and texture to get the look and feeling you want in your landscape.

The next factor you need to consider is the amount of water your plant choices need to grow and thrive. All plants need water, some more than others. If you want a xeriscape or low-maintenance landscape and you choose water-loving trees or plants, they will die. Insufficient water is the number one cause of death in plants and trees here in Central Oregon. We have seen it time and time again. If you don't want to water much, your plant choices are more restricted and you will need to use mostly native or wild types of trees and plants. Having an irrigation system dramatically widens your choices in plant material. Knowing the water requirements of your plant choices will allow you to adjust your irrigation system or watering schedule to provide optimal growing conditions for the plants and trees you choose.

Knowing where to buy is almost as important as what to buy. Your local nursery, preferably one that has been in business in your area for many years, is your best bet for getting the appropriate plant material and accurate information on care and planting. Box stores like Home Depot expect to lose money on their plants. They sell these "loss leaders" to draw in customers, who then spend money on other products. The plants they stock come from all over the country and are not necessarily rated to our climate here in Central Oregon. They buy the plants not because they'll thrive here, but because they got a good wholesale price on them. Then they sell those plants to customers who don't know any better. Usually their staff doesn't know any better either, so you won't be able to find out much of anything about how the plants grow or how to care for them. Indeed, a number of the state's top nurseries with the best plants won't even sell to box stores. So while the plants you buy at these stores may seem like a great deal at the time, how great a deal are they if they die after you've taken the time and effort to plant them? Even if the box store gives you your money back, you have still wasted time and effort, and are now back at square one with your planting.

In addition, a lot of the plants from these big box stores are grown in hot houses and have never been exposed to the outdoors. These plants are not on schedule with the season outside, and so are not able to handle the stress of suddenly being exposed to the elements for the first time. Consequently they wilt, shrivel and die. Plants need to be acclimated to the area if they are not grown here. They need to spend increasing amounts of time outside, exposed to heat, cold, wind, rain etc., in order to be in sync with the season and to handle the climate conditions. Putting plants and trees through this process is called "hardening," and hardened plants and trees fare vastly better than those that are not.

Now the fun begins! With your new understanding of the fundamentals in plant selection, you can indulge your artistic sensibilities. The final consideration in choosing plants is what Sarah calls the Four Season Landscape. You want your landscape to look its best winter, spring, summer and fall. Being an artist, she looks at a landscape like a canvas. She sees the trees and plants as the paint. Like Sarah, when you plant your garden you're painting in three dimensions and in four seasons. Instead of being static, the canvas and the paint are a dynamic flux of sizes, shapes, colors and textures that change with the seasons.

Winter is perhaps the most challenging season for a landscape to look good. Your evergreen choices are key. Begin with the evergreen trees and shrubs such as pines, spruce, cedars, Manzanita, Mugo Pine, etc. These plant materials will be more constant in appearance. They will grow, but will keep their color, leaves and needles year-round. Wherever you need year-round coverage choose an evergreen, which also requires less pruning and maintenance.

Evergreens can outline the basic structure and flow of your landscape throughout the year, and then you can fill in with the ever-changing colors and textures of the deciduous trees, shrubs and perennials. Annuals and perennials die back and offer almost nothing in winter, but deciduous shrubs and trees, even without the leaves, still give shape and structure. The bare branches contrast starkly and beautifully with the white snow, and sparkle and glisten with a cover of frost. The bark of some deciduous trees and woody shrubs provides color in winter. For example, the colored stems of Redtwig and Yellowtwig Dogwoods are much more apparent without the leaves, and really stand out against the snow or drab browns and grays of grass and other plants in winter. Sprinkle some of these types of plants throughout your landscape to liven up your winter garden.

Ah, spring. The earth begins to wake up after the long winter. The deciduous trees begin to leaf out, flowering trees blossom, flowers start to bloom and the grass slowly turns green again. Flowering trees and some shrubs are mainly spring bloomers. Spread these flowering plants and trees throughout your landscape, or concentrate them for impact in areas where you spend your time, like around your patio or back porch. Plant them where you can enjoy the color and fragrance wafting in through open windows or out on your deck.

Summer in Central Oregon is hot and the need for shade can be important. Broadleaf trees are great for shade in summer and for letting light in during winter. These types of trees and shrubs show terrific variety in the size, shape and texture of their leaves. Use this variety to create interest and flow from one area to another in your landscape. The predominant color of summer is green; however some trees and shrubs have colored leaves. Shrubs like barberry and sand cherry have red leaves, as do trees like Thundercloud Flowering Plum and Red Choke Cherry. Some shrubs, like Gold Mound Spirea, have yellow leaves. And summer is the heyday for many, many annuals and perennials that bloom all season long.

Fall is Sarah's personal favorite. She loves the brilliant reds, yellows and oranges of the trees and shrubs at this time of year. Aspen, Birch and Poplars, golden Ginkgos and Honey Locusts provide the yellows. The oranges often come from the Swedish Aspen and the Autumn Blaze and Sugar Maples. The Reds, of course, are found in Red Maple, Vine Maple, Burning Bush, Mountain Ash and the deep hues of the Pin Oak, to name a few. Some trees even have purple leaves in the fall like Autumn Applause Ash and PJM Rhododendrons, whose leaves are green in summer and purple in fall and winter.

Plant these trees and shrubs of brilliant color where you can view and enjoy them. Remember, too, that the leaves will fall, so plant them in areas where you don't mind raking or leaving them lie as mulch and organic material that will enhance the soil.

Each season has its beauty. A carefully planned landscape with the right plant choices and placements can look great in all four seasons. But all your time and effort may be in vain if you do not plant properly!

Secret #7 *Planting recipe: Dig the hole twice as wide as the root mass (container or ball and burlap) and slightly deeper. Soak the hole with water. Drop in your tree or plant, and sprinkle Mycorrhizae fungus around the roots. Fill in around the root mass with a 50-50 mixture of compost and dirt. If the tree or plant is not on automatic irrigation, build a damn so waterings will soak deep into the roots. Lightly sprinkle fertilizer on top of the ground to jumpstart the plant. Later add compost or compost tea (a liquid form of compost). Most losses happen in the first year, so be sure to protect new trees from pests (deer, gophers, rabbits, etc...).*

Trees, shrubs and plants usually come to you in one of three forms: in a container, in a burlap ball (B&B), or bare root. Some planting instructions are the same for all three variations, some a bit different. Let's start with the commonalities.

First you must dig a hole. Remember to use your legs to dig – they're bigger than your arms. A sharp shovel also helps. If digging is difficult, you may need to wet or soak the area and let it sit overnight. If this doesn't soften the dirt up enough or you can't wait, dig a smaller pilot hole (with a bar or pick if necessary) at the center of your prospective hole. By first digging out the center to depth, the sides will begin to crumble allowing you to dig out the rest more easily.

You want to make the hole twice as wide as the container, ball or root mass. The depth of the hole should be the same depth as the dirt in the container or the top of the root ball. If it is a bare root tree or plant, you want the place where the roots start spreading laterally to be about two inches below the level of the soil surrounding your hole.

Tip *Here in Central Oregon our soil is usually so dry that after you remove the dirt from the hole it is a good idea to fill the hole with water. Let the water absorb into the dirt forming the hole for a few minutes. That way it will stay moister longer and when the roots start to grow out and the surrounding soil will not be so hard.*

If the tree or plant is in a container, you want the soil in the container to be moist, but not wet. If it is wet, the dirt will stick to the container, making it harder to get out. Conversely, if the dirt in the container is too dry, it may crumble and fall apart when removed from the pot, and you don't want that either. To ensure that the dirt is moist, water the tree or plant a day or two before you are ready to plant it.

If the tree or plant is small enough to pick up, support the plant at the top of the pot with one hand and tip it upside down. Thump the bottom of the pot with your other hand a couple of times. This should release the plant. If it is stubborn, lay the tree or plant on its side and roll the container back and forth while pushing down on it gently with your hand, then repeat the tip and thump. If it remains stuck, cut the pot off with a pair of pruners.

If you have a large tree in a container, place it on its side. Push down on the container and roll it back and forth at the same time. Then thump on the bottom of the container with the bottom of your foot or the back of your shovel. You should now be able to pull the tree out of the pot. Once you have the tree or plant out of the container, you want to break up the roots on the sides and bottom of the root mass. You can do this with your hands, with pruners, or with the blade of your shovel. Cut through any circling roots and break up any really dense masses of roots. Breaking up the roots allows them to spread out properly into the surrounding soil when you plant them.

When working with a B&B (burlap ball) tree or plant, you don't need to worry about breaking up the roots or removing the burlap. The burlap breaks down quickly once planted and the roots can grow through the burlap quite easily.

Myth #6 *You need to remove the burlap.*

It bears repeating. Despite the prevalent and absolutely false myth above, do *not* remove the burlap, as this damages the tree or plant. You want to keep the dirt around the roots and the root ball intact. The only thing you need to do with a B&B tree or plant is cut the strings binding it at the top of the root ball. Do not do this until it has been planted and watered. Once it has been safely tucked into the ground, clear away the dirt from the top of the ball and carefully cut and remove the strings. You may also cut away any extra burlap sticking out from the top, or simply fold it back and cover it with dirt.

Tip *If the root ball feels loose or unstable, you may leave the ball tied at the top for up to six months. That will give the roots a chance to begin growing into the surrounding soil and the tree or plant a chance to stabilize. You still must remove the strings eventually or they will constrict the growth of the trunk and the tree will suffer.*

Working with bare-root trees or plants can be a bit trickier. Bare-root trees or plants are usually only available in the spring and need to be planted quickly. If you cannot plant the same day you purchase bare-root trees or plants, you must keep the roots moist at all times by wrapping them in wet cloths, wet sawdust or compost. When you are ready to plant, examine the roots, making sure to trim off any that are broken or damaged. If you do not remove these damaged parts, they will rot in the ground, potentially attracting fungus and disease. Spread out the roots and make sure your hole is wide enough to comfortably accommodate them so that they're not bunched up or stuck together.

Soil amendment is critical. Here in Central Oregon, as we mentioned earlier, our soil is extremely poor. It contains no organic material or humus, which is decomposed plant and animal matter. Our soil is also pH neutral. PH measures the acid or alkaline level of a substance. PH is rated on a scale of zero to fourteen, zero to six being acidic and eight to fourteen being alkaline. Our soil is right in the middle at seven, therefore pH neutral. Central Oregon soil composition basically consists of sand, rock, dust and pumice. It drains very rapidly and does not retain moisture. Amending the soil serves three main functions: it helps the soil retain moisture, it helps soften the soil so new roots can grow more easily and it provides nutrient value to the tree or plant as it continues to decompose.

Amending the soil with compost is a must. You want to use a good compost mixture. You can buy compost at the store or at a landscape supply company (I like the *Garden Mix* from Instant Landscape), or you can make a mixture yourself. Good compost is made from partially decomposed organic materials like grass, leaves, fruit and vegetable waste, and often some type of manure from grazing animals. (Waste from meat-eating animals is not used; dog poop is not an option.) If you have your own source of manure, make sure it is old and has been turned over several times. Fresh manure is HOT and can burn the roots of your plants. You can mix your manure with chopped-up leaves and grass clippings, or buy a bag of steer manure and a bag of peat moss or coconut fiber and mix them together.

Sarah likes to go one step further and add Mycorrhizae fungus to the mixture of dirt and compost. Mycorrhizae fungus is a filament-like fungus that has a symbiotic relationship with the roots of trees, and promotes the growth of fibrous roots on the tree. The fibrous roots are the very important, smaller, finer roots used for extracting and absorbing water and nutrients from the soil. The more fibrous roots the tree possesses, the hardier and more drought resistant it becomes.

Sarah first learned about this beneficial fungus while getting her Master Gardener certification. In class, the students saw roots of trees planted with and without Mycorrhizae fungus . The difference in the amount of fibrous root on the Mycorrhizae fungus trees was stunning. In Central Oregon, with our soil and climate conditions, our trees need every advantage they can get. Using Mycorrhizae fungus gives us healthier, more vigorous trees.

Mycorrhizae fungus usually comes in two forms: wet and dry. The wet form is a concentrate that you mix with water to form a dip used for bare-root trees and shrubs. The dry form is comprised of granules that you can mix in with your dirt and compost and put right into the hole around the roots of the tree or plant. The Mycorrhizae fungus must be next to the roots; it will not work if you sprinkle it on top of the dirt after planting.

Okay. You have your compost, your Mycorrhizae fungus and your pile of dirt from digging your hole.

Now mix them together. Sarah likes at least a 50-50 mixture of dirt and compost, and depending on the size of your tree a handful or two of the Mycorrhizae fungus granules. For container and B&B trees or plants, take a portion of your mixture and place it in the bottom of the hole you dug, spreading it out so it fills the bottom of the hole. Carefully place your tree or plant in the hole on top of the mixture. Make sure the top of the root mass or root ball is even with the surrounding soil level. Fill in around the sides of the root mass and press gently. Do not stomp on the fill mixture; you want air space in with the dirt-compost-Mycorrhizae fungus mixture, so you do not want it too compacted. Cover over the top of the root mass with no more than two to three inches of the mixture. Use extra dirt and compost to mound up around the sides of the hole to form a well or moat around the edges. This will make it easy to water the tree or plant and will keep the water from running off and away from where you want it.

Back to the bare-root tree or plant, the planting instructions are slightly different for this one. Take about half of the compost-dirt mixture and make a triangular mound in the bottom of the hole, then drape the roots down the outside of the mound. Once you have the roots around the outside of the mound, make sure the tree or plant is straight up and fill in and press down the mixture on top and around the roots. You may need to press a bit more firmly with a bare-root in order to get it to stay up straight. The area where the roots start branching from the main stalk or trunk should not be more than three inches below the ground level. Make a well around the edges of the hole with extra compost-dirt mixture, as we described above with the container and B&B trees or plants. If it is a large plant or tree it is best to have someone help you. One of you can hold the tree and the other can fill in the remaining mixture around the roots.

Now that your tree or plant is planted in the ground, it is time to apply fertilizer. Fertilizer consists of three main components; each fulfills a different nutrient function in promoting healthy growth of the tree or plant. The components of the fertilizer are always listed in the same order: nitrogen (N) first, then phosphorus (P), then potassium (K). Nitrogen provides for the growth of foliage, stems and trunk. (Be careful with this, however, as too much can burn foliage and grass.) Phosphorus is important for flower and fruit production and spreading of roots, and potassium helps maintain cell integrity, as well as the firmness of the tree or plant. If there are other components in the fertilizer, they will be listed after the three main components of N, P, and K. When it comes to choosing fertilizer, Sarah recommends a balanced blend, with equal amounts of each element, like N=10, P=10, K=10, otherwise known as triple 10 for trees and shrubs. Lawns like higher levels of nitrogen. Look for ratios of 3:1:2 or 4:1:2 (N=3 or 4, P=1, K=2). Soil microbes don't like fertilizers over 10.

A lot of people ask whether it is better to use organic or commercial fertilizer for their tree or plant. Though Sarah used to think that this made no difference to the plant or tree, she learned otherwise this year at the Farwest Nursery Show in Portland. A seminar on soil science taught her that Mother Nature already has a system in place; by using organic fertilizers we can work with that system and strengthen it. When we use commercial fertilizers on a frequent basis, we can actually damage or destroy the system. Here is how it works. There is a web of relationships between the tree or plant and the soil and the microscopic creatures that live in the soil. The system starts with the roots of the trees and plants, where the activity takes place. This root zone is called the rhizosphere. The roots secrete chemical compounds into the soil that attract and feed microscopic bacterial and fungi. These microbes in turn break down organic compounds in the soil and release nutrients for the tree or plant. The microscopic fungi and bacteria are also food for other microbes protazoa and nematodes who eat them and produce waste in the form of nutrients that the tree or plant can absorb. The protazoa and nematodes in turn are food for tiny arthropods (insects) which in turn are food for larger arthropods like crickets, silverfish and the like, which in turn are food for larger creatures like birds and rodents, and so on as the food chain continues, eventually reaching all the way to you and me.

In addition, when the microbes and arthropods die and decompose, they release more nutrients for the trees and plants. This is *The Soil Food Web* – Mother Natures's intricate and amazing system, which ensures a continuous supply of nutrients for the trees and plants. Not only do these beneficial microbes feed the trees and plants, they also extend the range of the roots, bring additional water to the roots, and surround and protect the roots from root eating pests and parasites.

When we use compost and Mycorrhizae fungus fungus (mentioned in our planting recipe), along with organic fertilizers, we promote the health and growth of the soil food web and help our trees and plants to feed themselves. When we use commercial chemical fertilizers, we kill many of these beneficial microbes and degrade the health of the soil food web. It is sort of like the old parable: give a man a fish and he will be fed that day; teach a man to fish and he can feed himself for life. Give the tree or plant some commercial fertilizer ... good for a short time or cultivate good soil and the soil food web and the trees and plants are fed continuously.

Also, the making of commercial fertilizer produces more waste and strain on the environment, whereas the production of organic fertilizer reduces waste and stress on the environment. The choice relates as much to your environmental conscience as to the long-term needs of your tree or plant.

Fertilizer goes on top of the ground. Take a handful, small or large depending on the size of the tree or plant, and sprinkle it around the base of the tree or plant. Do not put fertilizer in the hole; it is very concentrated and can burn the roots. Dissolving it by watering allows it to filter down through the dirt to the roots for optimal nutrient absorption.

Always fertilize new plantings. One exception to this rule is if you have a sensitive native species like Manzanita or Penstemons. For these types of native plants, Sarah uses only the compost mixture. Organic fertilizer, compost or compost tea can be re-applied throughout the growing season for optimal growth of your tree or plant; every three months works well.

Once the ground is frozen in late fall, fertilizing should stop, as the frozen ground prevents absorption. Fertilizing can resume in the spring once the ground is soft again. If you feel that fertilizing every three months is too much work, the minimum would be once in spring or once in the fall.

Water your newly planted tree or plant thoroughly. Fill up the well you made and let it soak in. Your mixture of dirt and compost will sink down a little. If it sinks down too far exposing the root mass or ball, add more mixture and water again. Fill up the well and let it soak in a couple of times to make sure the tree or plant is wet and fully covered. Watering will also help dissolve some of the fertilizer and make it available to the tree or plant. Keep your tree or plant moist at all times for the first two weeks. If you have an irrigation system in place, check to make sure your new tree or plant is getting good coverage. Vigilance with watering new plants pays off by reducing stress and helping them get established more quickly.

Newly planted trees and shrubs can be vulnerable in ways that established plantings are not. Here in Central Oregon, we have a substantial threat from deer and rodents. It is awful to wander out in your yard to inspect your newly planted tree and find that the bark has been stripped or chewed through by one of these pests. If you know there are deer in your area, you must take precautions. If unsure whether or not deer inhabit your area, protect your plantings anyway. It's not worth the risk. While caging trees and shrubs may not be visually appealing, unless your yard is completely enclosed with a six-foot high fence, you need to implement protection for your trees and shrubs. Sarah recommends using rigid plastic tree guards or taping the trunks of new trees for at least two years. After this time period, the plant materials have an established root system and the deer and other animals have gotten used to them being part of the landscape. For some reason deer in particular love to attack the new additions to a landscape. After your trees or plants have been there for a while they seem to leave them alone.

Chicken wire can be very effective for seedling trees (two- to three-feet tall or less), and for shrubs. Wrap the chicken wire around the tree or shrub forming a tube; use a cord or zip tie to close up the top and bottom of the wire around the seedling or shrub. The completed result should be a wire bubble around the plant. This leaves room for the tree or plant to grow but protects it from any substantial damage.

If you absolutely cannot stand the idea of caging your plants, there are some good deer repellents out there, but they need to be applied in the right conditions and re-applied every six to eight weeks. Keep in mind that if you apply repellent and it rains later that day or the next, you're not covered. Most repellents need to dry and cure on the plant for forty-eight hours in order to be effective for the period indicated.

You'll know if you have gophers in your yard from the holes and piles of dirt on the surface of your yard. Gophers cause the most damage to the roots of new trees because they like to eat them. Moles can also make mounds of dirt, but they will be much less abundant and obvious than gophers. Moles provide a beneficial service by eating insects and insect larvae under the soil. They can damage roots unintentionally while seeking their food, but this damage is usually minor. Gophers, on the other hand, intentionally damage roots. If gophers are a problem there are a couple of routes you can take. When planting your tree or plant, you can line the hole with wire mesh or hardware cloth, or you can put poisoned grain in the hole with your dirt and compost. The gophers will usually choose the grain over the roots, eat it and die. You can also put the poisoned grain in any of the open holes you find in your yard, and go after them that way as well. Of course, if you don't want to kill these creatures, the wire mesh is your best bet.

You have taken time and care to choose the appropriate plant materials for the climate and the environment and purpose in your landscape. You have made the effort and used the right materials and techniques to plant and protect properly. Now you want to maintain your investments and see them grow strong, healthy and beautiful in your landscape. In order to achieve this goal you must first understand some important aspects of how trees or plants grow.

Fred’s Best Natives

Trees & Shrubs

- Ponderosa Pine - *Pinus ponderosa*
- Vine Maple - *Acer circinatum*
- Manzanita - *Arctostaphylos patula*
- Sage Brush - *Ceratoides lanata*
- Oregon Grape Holly - *Mahonia aquifolium*

Perennials, Grass & Groundcover

- Penstemons - *Penstemon (species)*
- Yarrow - *Achillea (species)*
- Fescue *Festuca ovina glauca*
- Indian Rice Grass - *Oryzopsis hymenoides*
- Knicknick - *Arctostaphylos uva-ursi*

Sarah's Favorite Imports

Broadleaf trees

- Swedish Columnar Aspen – *Populus tremuloidies columaris*
- Mountain Ash - *Fraxinus (species)*
- Sunburst Honey Locusts – *Gleditsia triacanthos*
- Norway Maple – *Acer planatanoidies*
- Palmatum Maple - *Acer palmatum*
- Lombardi Poplar - *Populous nigra*
- Thundercloud Flowering Plum - *Prunus cerasifera*

Conifer Trees

- French Blue Scots Pine -*Pinus sylvestris, var.french blue*
- Bristlecone Pine - *Pinus aristata*
- Weeping Atlas Cedar- *Cedrus*
- Hoopsai Spruce - *Picea hoopasai*

Shrubs

- Red Twig Dogwood -*Cornus alba*
- Burning Bush - *Euonymus alata*
- Lilac - *Syringia vulgaris*
- Barberry -*Berberis (species)*
- Spireas - *Spirea (species)*
- Russian Sage -*Perovskia atriplicifolia*

Perennials

- Echineaca - *Echinacea purpurea*
- Coreopsis - *Coreopsis tinctoria*
- Lavender -*Lavandula grosso*
- Heucheras - *Huechera (species)*

Groundcover & Grasses

- Wooly Thyme - *Thymus pseudolanuginosus*
- Lamium - *Lamium maculatum*
- Succulents – *Seedums & Delosperma*
- Feather Reed Grass - *Chalamagrotis x acutiflora*

Chapter 7

How Does Your Garden Grow?

To understand how to maintain your landscape, you need to know how trees and plants grow. Let's begin with basic anatomy.

Most of the trees and plants in our region have four main parts with which we will concern ourselves: the roots, stems or trunks, leaves, and flowers.

The roots, located below the soil, primarily serve to anchor trees and plants in the soil and support the stems or trunk. Roots absorb water and nutrients from the soil and serve as storage units for the sugar (energy) the plant produces. Trees and plants have two main types of roots. The primary root grows long and down into the ground. The lateral or secondary roots grow out to the sides and branch off of one another and the primary roots. Some trees and plants have a very long primary root growing deep into the ground without much lateral branching; this root is called a tap root. Some of our native trees like the Ponderosa Pine have a tap root. The tap root gives the tree added stability and allows it to reach deep into the ground for water. Tap root trees such as the Ponderosa work great in dry climates like Central Oregon, but they are difficult to transplant. We get a lot of calls from clients who try to dig up and move Ponderosas only to have them die.

Tip *Trees with tap roots must be root pruned and allowed to recover in the ground by growing more lateral and fibrous roots in order to transplant successfully. Assuming you've root pruned in the fall, your tree will be ready for transplanting the next spring.*

The lateral roots of trees in particular spread out sideways and may extend for considerable distances, even beyond the edge of the foliage or "drip line" of the tree. The lateral roots don't extend as deeply in the ground; usually they spread out within the top one to two feet of soil. The lateral roots contain most of the fibrous roots or "feeder roots" with root hairs that absorb water, nutrients and minerals from the soil.

Tip *Because lateral roots are closer to the surface they are more likely to be damaged by construction, herbicides, pesticides and lawn maintenance equipment. To keep your trees healthy and alive, give the roots of large trees adequate room when planning your landscape and make room for existing trees when excavating for construction.*

Loose, well-drained soil amended with organic material (good compost) provides optimal conditions for healthy roots. As we discussed earlier in the planting section, our soil here in Central Oregon contains little to no organic material. This material is necessary because it contains soil microbes that break down fertilizers and nutrients in the compost into forms that trees and plants can absorb through their roots. You want the soil to be loose because roots need air as well as water. Heavily compacted soil cannot trap air and doesn't allow water to penetrate effectively either. Soil that is too wet and soggy also pushes out the air and makes roots slimy, rotten and unable to absorb nutrition. Burying a trees or plant too deeply in soil or covering it with too much bark or mulch can also suffocate the roots, preventing air and nutrients from effectively reaching them.

Tip *Never put more than two to three inches of bark or mulch around the base of trees and plants. Soil balanced with air, water, and organic material including soil microbes creates healthy well-functioning roots.*

The trunk, stems, stalks and branches of trees and plants give structure and support, and house the vascular system of the organism. Much like our own circulatory system, the vascular system moves water and nutrients to different areas, as needed throughout the tree and plant. Like us, trees and plants have two kinds of vascular tissue. We possess veins and arteries; trees and plants possess xylem and phloem. These tissues can be equated to thousands of tubes or straws bundled together inside the trunks, stems and branches. The xylem is the inner layer of vascular tubes that flow in one direction only. This inner layer carries water and dissolved nutrients from the roots up to the leaves. As a tree grows, the innermost layers of the xylem stop carrying fluids and become what we call the heartwood or pith. The layers of the xylem that are still active inside the tree are called the sapwood. The phloem tubes wrap around the xylem tubes and are separated by a very thin layer of tissue. The phloem can flow in both directions, taking the sugars produced in the leaves and moving them throughout the tree and plant to roots, stems, flowers or fruits, wherever that tree or plant needs energy to perform its various seasonal functions.

The thin layer of tissue separating the xylem and phloem is called the cambium layer. The cambium layer is where the tree or woody shrub grows thicker. On the inside, the cambium produces new xylem tissue and on the outside it produces new phloem tissue. This very important tissue-producing cambium lies quite close to the surface, just underneath the phloem and the bark.

Tip *Young trees have very thin bark that is easily scraped or chewed through by deer and rodents. If the cambium layer is damaged around more than half the circumference of the trunk, the production of xylem and phloem and the flow of nutrients and energy will be so compromised that the tree will die.*

This tender young bark explains why protecting the trunks of young trees for at least their first two years is of such paramount importance. As trees age their bark becomes thick, rigid and often rough and bumpy, providing much more protection from the assaults of various animals. The thick bark of many varieties of mature trees can even withstand forest fires.

The top of trees and shrubs containing most of the leaves and branches is called the crown. Buds on trees and plants control and regulate the growth of the crown. Buds located at the ends of stems and branches are called terminal buds. Ancillary buds are those located on the sides of the branch or stem usually in an axil, which is where leaves and stem meet on a branch. The terminal bud controls the axillary buds by emitting a hormone, which to a certain extent suppresses the growth of the other buds. We will discuss this further when we get into pruning. For now it is enough to know that the crown grows outward from the terminal buds.

Trees and plants are unique organisms because they can make their own food. Their leaves are the energy factories; they capture sunlight using the green pigment chlorophyll which is located in special cells called chloroplasts. Inside the chloroplasts, sunlight combines with water brought up from the roots and carbon dioxide from the atmosphere (also absorbed through the leaves) to make sugar. This process of converting light, water and carbon dioxide into energy is called photosynthesis. You probably remember that much from your high school biology class. If any one of these three components goes missing or is not available in adequate amounts, the process of photosynthesis stops. If it stops for too long, trees and plants will starve and die.

Tip *Around here, water is usually the ingredient that goes missing or falls short of the adequate amount. If hand-watering, use Soil Moist granules to help your trees and plants retain moisture in between waterings.*

Leaves also serve two other important functions for the tree or plant. The first, respiration, involves the digesting or breaking downs of the sugars made during photosynthesis. Basically, this entails burning the energy the plant has produced. The byproduct of burning this energy—oxygen—is released back into the atmosphere. As humans and animals, we depend on oxygen to survive, which means that our survival depends on this symbiotic relationship with trees and plants. Transpiration, the leaves' other function, involves the release of water vapor into the atmosphere. Trees and plants transpire water vapor in order to keep them cool and to maintain cell integrity or firmness by regulating fluid within the cell membranes. Special pores on the underside of the leaves, called stomata, open and close to facilitate transpiration. The amount of water vapor released relates directly to temperature, humidity and wind in the surrounding environment. As you can see, leaves are vital organs of the tree and plant.

Beautiful, colorful and often sweet-smelling, we come to the flowers. Flowers are all about sex. Flowers contain the male and female sexual organs of trees and plants. Some contain both male and female parts in the same flower, some have separate male flowers and female flowers on the same tree or plant and some species have only male flowers on one tree or plant and only female flowers on the other. Some flowers don't even look like flowers—the pine cone, for example, is actually a female flower.

Facilitation of sexual reproduction is the flower's primary function. For trees and plants, sex means pollination: the transfer of the pollen containing the male genetic material to the ovule containing the female genetic material. The many various forms, colors and shapes of flowers facilitate pollination, or more to the point facilitate pollinators. Pollinators can be insects, birds or animals, and for many trees and plants the wind does the job. You've probably read or seen nature programs describing some of the intricate, evolved relationships between plants and their pollinators, where the flowers' shape, color or scent is designed specifically to attract the preferred bird, butterfly or beetle to pollinate them. Pollinators carry the pollen from one flower or plant to the next and ensure transfer of the genetic material. Once the pollen is successfully delivered to the ovule, fertilization takes place and the ovule becomes a viable seed that can grow into an entirely new tree or plant of the parent species.

Ovules (or eggs) reside in the ovary. When seeds become viable, the ovary grows a fleshy covering around them: fruit. Apples, pears, cherries, tomatoes, squash, etc. are fleshy ovaries surrounding their seeds. Fruit serves a couple of purposes. It protects the seeds, often providing a medium in which the germinating seed can grow. Fruits also increase the disbursement of seeds. Since they taste good, they're consumed by many animals, which then carry the seeds to new locations before excreting them as waste. These excreted seeds can then germinate and grow into new trees and plants.

Of course, fruits are not the only edible parts of plants; we also eat the leaves like lettuce, kale, etc., and the roots like carrots, potatoes, etc. Once again trees and plants support us by providing tremendous amounts of food products we humans depend on to live. When given a closer look, the ingenuity inherent in our trees' and plants' anatomy, growth, food production and reproduction truly amaze.

Now that you understand some of the tree and plant structures and methods of living and growing, you can work in harmony with their systems to manage and maintain your landscape.

Chapter 8

Pruning Primer

Many of Sarah's clients are nervous or unclear about when and why to prune. As a result, they—like a lot of people—wait until their trees and plants are overgrown and out of control before they start pruning. Then they hack away haphazardly, often doing more harm than good. Pruning should be done for specific reasons and results.

Pruning directs or limits growth and maintains the health of plants and trees. Directing growth controls where the trees and plants send their energy. During the first few years of a plant's or tree's growth, we prune to direct growth by removing stems and branches that do not structurally contribute to the desired mature shape. Directing growth can also improve the size and quality of fruit and flowers. Later, trees and plants can be pruned to limit their growth, and therefore their size. (In Bonsai, which includes pruning roots, this limiting of size is taken to the extreme.) At all times, trees and plants need to be pruned to keep them healthy. This entails removing dead or disease-infested branches and stems.

The first few years of a new landscape require the most attention and direction from you. The first growing season after planting, most trees and plants spend their energy getting rooted. They really start to take off the second through the fourth seasons, during which time they can produce a lot of growth. You want to train and direct this growth to achieve the desired healthy look of the mature landscape goals. Pruning will play a major role in the structural, formative care of a new landscape. In a mature landscape, or once the landscape has grown in, pruning will be used for health and maintenance only.

Most broadleaf deciduous trees, and evergreen trees (birch, maple, ash, aspen, poplar, apples, oak, pine spruce, fir etc.) should be pruned in late winter.

Tip *Evergreens especially should never be pruned during warm months when their sap is flowing, because flowing sap entices pestilent moths to lay their eggs on the trees. Their larvae—boring grubs—eat into the tree under the bark, causing damage to the tree.*

Pruning from mid-February to mid-March works well as a general rule. Cherry, plum, peach and apricot are an exception to this rule. Their bark is prone to splitting and should be pruned in June when the overall temperature is warmer. A number of shrubs, like rhododendron, azalea and forsythia, bloom on last year's growth, so wait until about a month after they bloom before pruning if you want to enjoy the flowers.

Tip *A good rule of thumb for these kinds of shrubs is that if the flowers come before the leaves, they are* *blooming on last year's growth. If the flowers come after the leaves, they are blooming on this season's growth.*

Deciduous trees in general benefit from an open center with strong, well-spaced branches. You want to start at the bottom and work your way up the tree. At the base of the trunk where it meets the ground, locate and remove any suckers or sprouts growing out from the base of the tree. We want the energy of the tree to go upwards into the branches.

Tip *The only reason not to remove suckers is if you want to turn a single trunk into a clump or multiple. In some trees like Aspen or Birch, the clump is a natural tendency of the tree and may be desirable. If this is the case, keep two to three of the most substantial shoots and remove all others.*

Now move up the trunk removing any shoots or branches that are lower than the desired trunk height. The height of the trunk is usually three to four feet from the ground to the starting point of the major branches of the canopy. In columnar trees, the main branching starts between one to two feet from the ground.

When you get to the branches, walk around the tree and examine the spacing of the major branches. Usually you'll find a central leader continuing up from the trunk with the major branches growing out laterally. The central leader is particularly easy to see in evergreens; it is the central pole of the tree from which all the major branches extend. In deciduous trees, the central leader is sometimes missing and two to three major vertical branches will grow up from the trunk instead. These major vertical branches then become the leaders, on which the lateral branches will grow out to the sides.

The lateral branches should be evenly spaced from one to two feet apart as they spiral up the central leader or leaders from the trunk. The minor branches then fill in the space between the majors. For deciduous trees, branches crowded together with less than ten inches between them side to side or top to bottom should be removed until you achieve even spacing around the trunk with between five to eight major lateral branches.

A healthy branch is a strong branch. The angle of the crotch (where the branch meets the trunk) can be no less than 45 degrees for a branch to have proper strength. Branches with narrow crotch angles less than 45 degrees frequently break in wind or ice storms. Branches with angles from 55 to 75 degrees are strongest.

Tip *You don't have to carry a protractor with you; just make a peace sign with your first two fingers. If the crotch angel is narrower than that, the branch should be removed.*

Now look inside the canopy. The area around the central leader should be open, so that air and light can get in. Remove any branches growing in toward the central leader. Remove any branches rubbing against each other or along a major branch. Branches growing down instead of up can also be removed. If there are broken or diseased-looking branches, prune those back to the next healthy intersecting branch or to the trunk if necessary. Diseased branches look different from healthy branches in color—usually black to grayish and darker than healthy bark—and the bark appears shriveled, sometimes peeling or cracking. If a branch has broken close to the trunk, remove it all the way to the trunk. One other type of branch to watch for and remove is called a water sprout. These sprouts grow straight up from a horizontal branch, trying to occupy the opened center, often looking greener and feeling softer than a normal branch. Not structurally as strong as normal branches, they often shoot up after an initial pruning in spring.

Young trees and shrubs can often be leggy, with only a few long stems or leading branches, and without much lateral or secondary branching. They look wispy or gangly. To get trees and shrubs to push out lateral growth, you must cut off the terminal buds at the ends of the branches. Generally you want to keep a central leader; this is especially true for evergreens, like pine, spruce and fir. As we've noted, deciduous trees may have from one to three major vertical branches. Shrubs usually have three or more main stems as well. You want to keep the other major branches from competing with the central leader or leaders. Cut them back about twelve to eighteen inches from the tip to the next intersecting branch, bud or leaf intersection. The terminal bud, as we briefly mentioned earlier, produces a hormone that suppresses growth of the buds below. Gravity carries the hormone downward from the tip of the branch. Removing the terminal bud stops the production of the hormone, setting the axillary buds free to push out laterally until new terminal buds form on the ends of the new branches. This type of cut is called a "heading" cut. This process may be repeated every other year, until the desired shape and fullness of the crown or canopy is achieved.

Deciduous shrubs may increase the number of stems each year. "Thinning" cuts remove extra stems and branches. If you want your shrubs to grow taller, have fewer stems. Cut lesser stems back to the ground or base of the plant, and cut the terminal buds less often. If you want bushier shrubs, keep more of the stems and cut back the terminal buds to the nearest bud or leaf intersection to encourage lateral branching from the selected stems.

Thinning is also used to improve the size and quality of flowers and fruit. For flowering shrubs, more branches means more flowers; and fewer stems and branches can give fewer, but bigger, flowers. This is often the case with roses. For annuals and perennials, pinching off the dead flowers throughout the growing season keeps many plants blooming longer. For better fruit, you want to wait until after flowering to thin, first because you want the blossoms pollinated and second because it's easier to see what you've got. Once the flowers fall off, you will soon start to see very small fruits (miniature apples, pears, plums etc.) forming at the end of stems growing out of small spurs off the branches. Say you have an apple tree, and you see many mini apples growing off of one spur. For good sized apples you want to leave only two to three mini apples on the spur; so pick the best looking minis and carefully snip the stems of extras.

The tree will then send all of its energy into the remaining minis and produce larger fruit.

Directing growth in evergreen trees and shrubs requires considerably less pruning than deciduous trees and plants. Evergreens grow more slowly to begin with, and naturally more or less maintain their initial shape. The branches of evergreen trees occur in relatively evenly spaced rings or whorls on the central leader reflecting each year's growth. Examine the whorls of branches where they attach to the trunk. They will be more closely spaced than the branches of a deciduous tree. The smaller the tree, the closer together they will be. As the central trunk thickens, the space between the branches on each whorl will spread out. Only if the whorl of branches is extremely crowded should you remove a very few branches at the trunk. The ends of the branches grow out laterally in regular-sized segments each year as well. In spring, candles shoot up from buds at the ends of the branches. These candles initially grow long, sometimes a foot or longer, and then push out their needles. To make the tree bushier and branch out more, wait until the candles extend. While they're still soft and before you see the needles starting to poke through, cut the candle at half its length at a 45 degree angle with your pruners. The angle of the cut will keep excess moisture and pitch from accumulating and the cut will heal faster.

Evergreen trees such as pines naturally become more open and woody in the center. Denser evergreens like spruce, fir and evergreen shrubs can accumulate dead branches and needles in their center that need to be cleaned out regularly. Some of the lower branches of evergreen trees and shrubs naturally die off as they grow taller. These should be removed to keep the trunk and base clean.

Tip *Clearing away debris like branches needles and leaves from the base of trees reduces infestation from pests and disease, and minimizes damage to the tree and surrounding soil should a fire occur.*

Due to the natural pyramidal shape of evergreen trees, they need a strong central leader to maintain their shape. If the central leader is broken on damaged, it must be removed and replaced. Cut it back to just above the next whorl of limbs below it. Take a branch from that whorl and carefully bend it up in place of the leader. Using a stick or dowel for added support, tape it to the trunk below the cut and tape the new branch you bent up to the stick above the cut. Leave it taped for six months. Eventually it will take over as the new leader and keep the natural pyramidal shape on track.

The other two reasons for pruning—limiting growth and promoting health—use the same types of pruning cuts we have already discussed. Limiting growth is used to maintain size of a shrub or tree. Once you have achieved the size and shape desired, you prune to keep that look by *thinning* (cutting out extra branches and stems), and by *heading* (removing terminal buds). In evergreens you would remove the new candle completely where it connects to the branch, stopping the growth for that season. When pruning for health, remember the three Ds: remove dead, diseased or damaged parts of the tree or plant as they occur.

Topping is a type of pruning you want to avoid. Trees that grow too close to power lines are often victims of topping. You have probably seen them; they look awful. You may have also seen it in Weeping Willows, huge old ones. Topping takes off a third to half (in severe cases) of the tree's major vertical central leaders and major branches, leaving stumps sticking up. This causes structural damage to the tree, and can even kill it. The branches that try to grow back on these stumps are like the water sprouts, not structurally strong, and easily broken in wind and storms. These trees never look normal or good again. Plant your trees away from power lines or use dwarf or semi-dwarf trees if you plant underneath power lines, and know the mature size of the tree before you plant it. This way you can avoid topping.

Now you know when, what and why to prune. Of equal importance is how to make the proper cuts and which tools to use when making them.

When making heading and thinning cuts always cut about a quarter inch above the next bud or leaf axil (intersection) on the branch or stem. If you cut just anywhere, instead of close to the junctures of leaf stems or buds, the cut piece left on the branch will die back to the nearest juncture anyway. This dead stub on the branch is both unattractive and a haven for pests and disease.

Unless you're cutting away a branch, cut on a 45 degree angle. This will allow the cut area to shed water and heal more quickly.

If you're removing an entire branch from the trunk or larger branch, you want your cut to be flush with the branch collar. The branch collar exhibits as thick ridges in circular formation around the base of the branch where it meets the trunk or next branch down. The bottom of the branch collar often pushes out a little more, forming a natural angle. Take your time to make the cut flush without cutting into the collar. The branch collar has the ability to naturally seal up the wound created by removing the branch. If you cut into the branch collar, you will damage it and the wound will not heal properly, leaving an opening for pests to invade.

If a branch is very large (more than three inches thick) and heavy you must make three separate cuts to avoid ripping and tearing caused by the weight of the branch. First, make a cut about twelve inches out from the branch collar. Cut half way through the branch from the top down. Second, make a cut three inches closer in toward the trunk. On this one, cut from the bottom up halfway through the branch. The branch will break where you have directed it, leaving a manageable stub. Now you can more easily make your cut flush with the branch collar.

The type of tool you use for the cutting relates most directly to the size of the branches or stems you want to remove. A good quality pair of handheld pruners work great for anything up to three-quarter-inch thickness. You want the scissor-action style, rather than the anvil style pruners. The scissor style has two sharp, curved blades, one of which cuts from the bottom up and the other from the top down. The anvil has a sharp, flat blade on top that comes down on to a wider flat plate, sometimes with little teeth for gripping the branch. The anvil can crush a branch while cutting it, causing rough edges and a poor cut. The scissor-action hand pruners cut cleanly and smoothly, so they're easier on you and the branch.

The next size up, three-quarter-inch up to two-and-a-half-inch loppers, work wonderfully. Loppers have the same kind of blades as the scissor-action hand pruners, but they have long handles for more leverage and are operated with both hands. Close the blades of the loppers on the branch at the proper angle, then steadily push the handles toward each other to make the cut.

When wood dies it hardens and may be too much for the loppers. So the next tool on our list is the pruning saw, which is mostly available in three forms: foldable, regular and power saws. With the foldable type, you open the saw, tighten it with a nut to keep the blade out to use, and then close up to store. Sarah prefers the regular pruning saw that comes ready to use and can't collapse on her when cutting. Pruning saws have a fairly thin, long, sharp blade which makes it easy to get into tight spaces between branches. For cutting higher branches you can use a pole saw, basically a pruning saw on top of a long pole. Some pole saws also include a pruner that you engage to cut by pulling a cord that runs down the length of the pole. However, trying to make a good cut while hanging onto the bottom of a pole with the saw five feet away from you can be quite a challenge, and takes practice to do it well. Getting on a ladder allows you to get closer, so you can see what you are cutting.

One saw larger still, a bow saw, is only really needed for cutting down trees or very thick large branches. A bow saw is shaped like letter D, with the blade forming the straight line. These saws are light and cut easily, but do not fit into small spaces very well, so they have a limited versatility compared to a regular pruning saw.

Last and loudest, of course, you have chainsaws, some of which are electric and most of which are gas-powered. Chain saws are really not for pruning, they are for felling trees and cutting them into rounds. The only people who should be pruning with chain saws are professional tree trimmers who work on thirty- to one-hundred-foot mature trees. When they are high up in a big tree dangling from a rope, they need to do things quickly, so they use the chain saw. If you have trees this large in your landscape that need pruning, don't try it. Call a professional. It is very difficult and dangerous, and requires trained professionals to do a proper job.

You can do 99 percent of your pruning with the scissor-action hand pruners, loppers and a pruning saw. If you take good care of your tools, these will last you for years and years. Clean and oil your tools after using them, sharpen them regularly, and store them in a dry place. It is also important to clean your tools with antiseptic, like alcohol or a bleach solution in between pruning different trees and plants on your landscape. Cleaning prevents the spread of disease from one plant to the next. Get yourself a small spray bottle, some isopropyl alcohol or bleach diluted with an equal amount of water, and a cloth for wiping, and add those to your pruning tools. In between trees and plants, just spray the blades of the tools you used, wipe them off and you're ready to move on to the next plant.

Now you know the when, what, why and how, of pruning. It will take a while to get a feel for it. If you are shaping a shrub or tree, have a plan in mind of how the finished shape will look. Don't just start cutting and hope it will look right, as this generally leads to lopsided plants. If you are removing dead or diseased wood, you don't get a choice of not cutting or cutting less, but if you are pruning for shape you can be selective and keep an attractive look. So stand back, take a good look at the shrub or tree from all sides, and know what you are going for before you cut. Your trees and plants want the same things we all do: growth, health and good looks. Proper pruning will help fulfill those goals. The same is true when it comes to maintaining your garden in other ways.

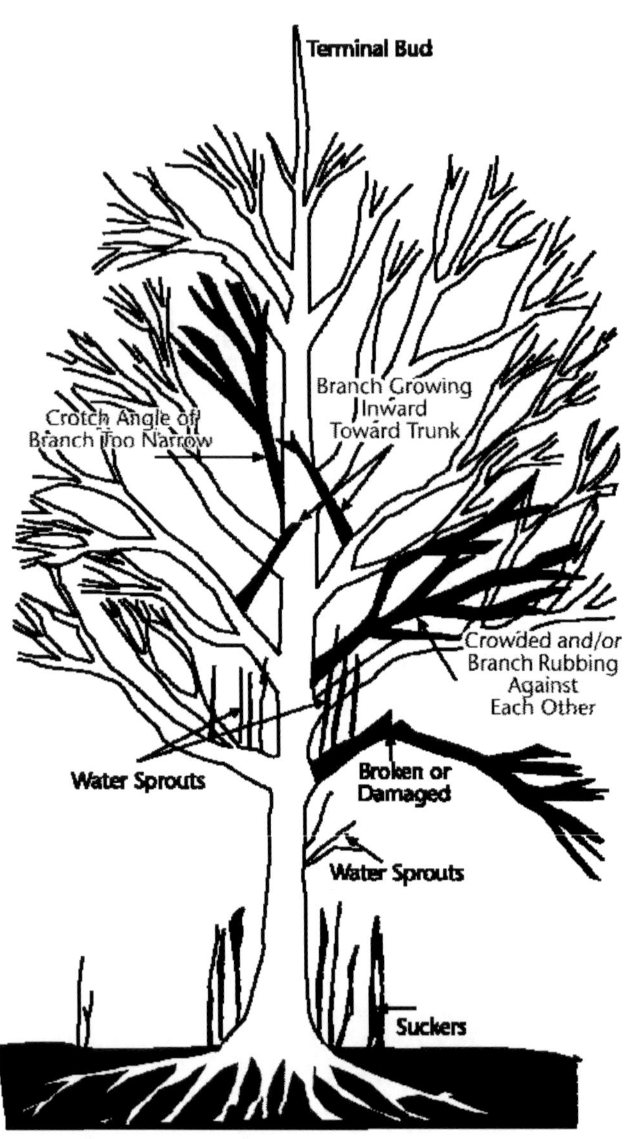
Terminal Bud
Branch Growing
Inward
Toward Trunk
Crotch Angle of
Branch Too Narrow
Crowded and/or
Branch Rubbing
Against
Each Other
Water Sprouts
Broken or
Damaged
Water Sprouts
Suckers

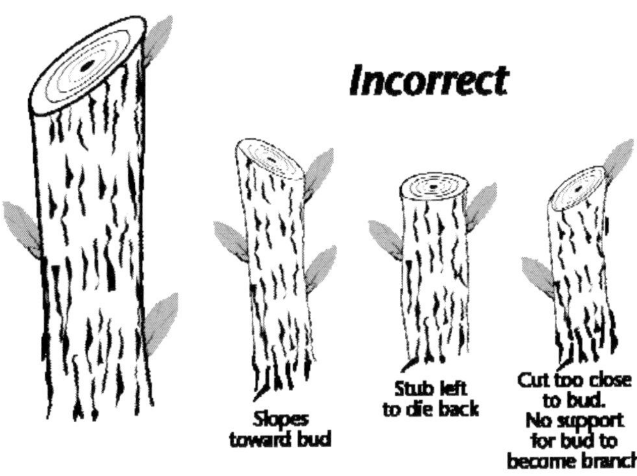
Correct
Incorrect
Slopes
toward bud
Stub left
to die back
Cut too close
to bud.
No support
for bud to
become branch

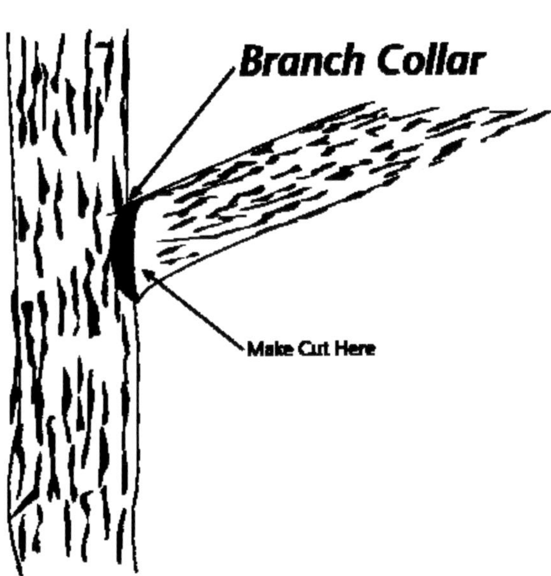
Branch Collar
Make Cut Here

Chapter 9

Maintaining Your Investment

Appropriate, regular maintenance will promote the health and longevity of your landscape. Whether you perform the maintenance duties yourself or hire a yard care service to do the work, you need to know what to do, as well as when and why specific maintenance tasks should be performed. Then you can be confident that you and/or your hired help are doing the right thing at the right time.

The duties of your landscape's maintenance are largely determined by the time of year. Your trees, plants and lawn change with the seasons and so do their maintenance requirements. This chapter will serve as your seasonal maintenance calendar.

Let's start with winter, the end of the old year and the start of the new. For the most part, we define winter in Central Oregon as December, January, and February. If this is your first winter in a new home or with a new landscape, or if you have an irrigation system, check to make sure the valve boxes are insulated. Unlike most of your system which is underground, parts of the pipes and the valves are exposed inside the box, so that you can use them. If they are not insulated, take some spongy foam-rubber or an old pillow or blanket, put it in a plastic bag and carefully push it down into the valve box and close it back up. This will protect your valves from cracking if it gets really cold.

Unless the weather is very mild, the only contact you need to make with your trees and shrubs during this time may be stringing some Christmas lights. When we don't receive much precipitation in the form of rain or snow, you will want to soak your trees and shrubs once their buds start pushing just before spring. Otherwise, your landscape will not need much attention from you during the months of winter. So kick back and enjoy the holidays; your landscape is giving you some time off.

About the last two weeks of February, you can prune your evergreens and most of your deciduous trees and shrubs. As indicated in the last chapter, you should be pruning for shape and removing branches and stems broken or damaged over the winter. (Refer to the previous chapter for how-to pruning specifics.) Pruning these kinds of trees in winter works best because that's when the sap of the tree, and therefore its energy, moves down into the roots and into the ground where it is warmer. During this form of hibernation, the tree's energy remains in the roots until spring. Once the average temperature rises, so does the sap. Pruning in late winter before the sap rises allows you to make pruning cuts that don't weep (i.e.: ooze sap). Pruning at this time is cleaner and better for the tree. That's pretty much all you need to do until spring.

During March, April and May, spring cleaning your landscape will start things off right. Winter has a tendency to accumulate debris such as leaves, branches and needles brought down by wind and snow. March is a good time for cleaning. Rake out your planter beds and lawn. If you didn't trim the dead plant material off of your perennials in fall do it now; this way the new growth for the season isn't encumbered by last season's dead or rotting leaves and stems. The same goes for ornamental grasses; you can pull out the dead grass and seed stalks.

Tip *Wearing dishwashing gloves works well for cleaning up your ornamental grasses. The rubber grips the dead grass more easily than cloth gloves, which let more dead grass slip through your grip.*

By mid March the ground is soft again, making it a good time to plant any spring bulbs like lilies and gladiolas (as opposed to fall bulbs like tulips, daffodils and hyacinths). You can also begin planting trees and shrubs again. This is also the time to transplant or move any trees or plants to a different location in your landscape. The ground this time of year in Central Oregon is usually quite moist from winter precipitation, so aside from watering them when you plant them, you do not need to be too concerned about keeping them watered until the weather gets warmer and drier toward the end of May. If you plan to seed native grasses or wild flowers in your landscape, do that in March as well.

Tip *When seeding wildflowers and native grasses, mix the seed in with good compost, then spread it and lightly rake it in to the soil. This gives the seed a little* *coverage and provides good material that will encourage germination and growth.*

If you have a lawn more than three years old, spring is a good time to thatch. If you have a new lawn, you don't have thatch. Thatch is dead grass from mowing that falls down in between the blades of the live grass. This material builds up over time and forms a thick matt, making it difficult for water and nutrients to penetrate, thereby minimizing their effect and stressing the health of the live grass. Thatch is removed by a machine; you can get one from an equipment rental place or have a lawn service come and do it for you. We recommend the latter; the thatching machines are heavy and unwieldy at best. Even if you have a catch bag on your mower, thatch can still build up over time. Thatching every two to three years will keep your lawn healthy.

You can also aerate your lawn from mid March through April. Over time soil compacts and prevents moisture, air and nutrients from reaching the grass roots effectively. This is especially true if your lawn gets a lot of use during the warm months of the year. Look for an aerating machine that pulls little plugs of grass and soil out of your lawn rather than one that pokes holes in the soil with spikes. The latter aerating machines are not as effective at breaking up the compaction and allowing air, water and nutrients to penetrate into the roots again. The plugs of lawn and dirt pulled out by the machine can be left on your lawn; they will dissolve back into the lawn in a short time.

Thatch first, then aerate. If you do it the other way around the newly softened soil will not bear the weight of the thatching machine, which can result in ripped up sections of your lawn. Aerating can also be done every two to three years. If you move into a home with an established landscape and the lawn looks like it has lost its vigor, thatching and aerating will prove a good start toward reviving the lawn.

Tip *Another treatment for lawn rejuvenation is to spread some good compost over your lawn and rake it in. This will improve the soil for the roots, provide beneficial microbes and nutrients and even protect your lawn from turf fungus. You can also throw compost and turf seed into any bare spots on your lawn this time of year.*

Once you've aerated your lawn, you'll want to fertilize it. Lawns need different fertilizers than trees, shrubs and perennials. Lawns like a three to one ratio of nitrogen (N) to phosphorus (P), and a two to one ratio of potassium (K) to phosphorus (P). So your best bet is a 3-1-2 ratio (N=3, P=1, K=2). Always water your lawn after fertilizing it, since the fertilizers that haven't been dissolved can burn the grass. If you do this early in spring before you have turned on your irrigation system, get out a hose-end sprinkler or spray it down by hand. You don't need to soak it; just get it wet and wash the fertilizer down into the lawn's roots.

Spring is also a good time to amend the soil in your vegetable garden with good compost. Turn over the soil and work it in thoroughly, so that it's ready to go once it's time to plant. You can also fertilize your trees and shrubs using a balanced fertilizer. This will get them off to a good start for blooming and leafing out.

April is also the time to start plants indoors. Tender herbaceous plants like flowers, herbs and vegetables need to grow in indoors for about eight to ten weeks before they can be transplanted outside. You can grow your flowers, herbs and vegetables from seed, sowing them in mid to late May. However, due to our short growing season, you will likely get more food from your garden if you start plants ahead of time indoors or in a greenhouse, or if you buy the plants from a nursery. By mid April you will want to turn on your irrigation system, or get out the hose and start watering. If we have a rainy spring, that can wait until May. Memorial Day weekend marks the official time for Central Oregonians to plant outside and hope for the most part anyway that the frosts are over. Summertime has arrived at last.

During the summer—June, July and August—the weather goes from warm to downright hot fairly quickly. Except for the occasional thunderstorm, summertime is also very dry. Making sure your trees and shrubs get plenty of water during summer keeps your landscape healthy. Examine your plants and trees periodically throughout the summer months; if they look wilted, or the leaves of your trees look limp or shriveled and dry, chances are they need more water. If you have irrigation, turn on your system and check to see if and where the water is spraying. Sprinkler heads and drippers can get clogged or knocked out of place. Make sure the water is going to the right spots. Also check sprinklers if you notice dry sections of your lawn. Ideally your lawn and your trees and shrubs are in different irrigation zones. Trees and shrubs benefit from longer periods of watering (twenty to thirty minutes) less often, and lawns like water more often, for shorter periods of time (ten to fifteen minutes). Spray head sprinklers, which broadcast water over large areas, work best for lawns, and bubblers or drip systems, which deposit water to a specific spot, usually work better for trees and shrubs. Street trees, which are often planted along sidewalks, may be planted in a lawn strip watered by spray-head sprinklers. In this case you can water this section a bit longer than you would if it were solely lawn. It is best to water lawn in the morning; watering at night can keep it damp for too long and may encourage fungus. Trees and shrubs are better watered in the late afternoon or evening, giving the water more time to soak into the soil and roots instead of evaporating in the heat of the day. So if you have an irrigation system, keep this in mind when setting your timer for your lawn and tree zones. If you don't, you now know when to drag out the hose for watering.

In early June you can finish pruning. Shrubs that bloom on last year's growth should be done blooming and ready to prune. If your shrubs don't need pruning, removing the dead flower heads after they finish blooming will keep them looking good. You can also prune your more cold-sensitive trees like cherries, apricots, and plums (see Chapter 7 for specifics) now. Roses can also be pruned at this time.

You may continue to plant trees, shrubs and perennials throughout the summer, but keep in mind that during the hot months plants are much more likely to suffer stress in the process. It really is preferable to plant in spring or fall. If you plant as many trees and shrubs as we do, you are bound to lose a few. Nine times out of ten, the ones that don't make it are the ones planted in the middle of summer and did not receive enough water. If you do choose to plant during the summer, you must be vigilant with the watering. Plant in the morning or evening, not in the heat of the day, and give the newly planted item extra water during the first two weeks to keep it from stressing during the hot months.

Summertime is also when pests and disease rear their ugly heads. Fortunately, our Central Oregon climate, with its cold winters and dry summers, keeps pests and disease to a minimum. However, they can still be an issue. In dealing with plant pests and disease, one of the most valuable lessons came to us from the State Department of Agriculture's Nursery Inspector. Every couple of years, the state of Oregon sends an inspector to look at our nursery. This particular year had been very warm, and Sarah had black spot and aphids all over her aspen trees. The chemical spraying did not seem to be working. The inspector explained about what he called the "Pathology Triangle," which consists of the *host*, the *environment*, and the *pathogen*. All three elements have to be working together for damage to occur to the tree or plant. By changing any side of the triangle, you can halt the disease of the plant in question.

In Sarah's case, over a hundred aspens were grouped very closely together, making it easy for the black spot fungus and the aphids to move from tree to tree. Also, because the trees were closely grouped, the moisture from watering never fully evaporated, thereby aiding the fungus. The leg of the triangle she needed to change was the environment. She separated her aspens into long lines that were only two to three across—instead of ten deep—so that more air could circulate among the leaves, allowing them to dry out between waterings. This change immediately decreased the infestation of the black spot fungus. To deal with the aphids, Sarah introduced a natural predator to the environment: She acquired some ladybugs. They made quick work of the aphids and her aspens were healthy again in no time.

We later saw the Pathology Triangle in action with a bark beetle infestation. Bark beetles of various types often attack pine trees and can cause trees to die. Though they rarely attack or damage healthy trees, since the latter have their own defense mechanisms, they'll bore into an already weakened and stressed tree and finish it off. But you can dramatically improve your tree's chances for survival by shifting a leg of the Pathology Triangle. Several years ago, Fred's parents had a big Ponderosa infested with bark beetles. It had been a dry winter and a hot summer, and the tree was feeling the stress. To try to save the Ponderosa, Fred suggested that his parents give the tree extra water and fertilize it. By improving the condition of the host, he figured the tree might save itself. His folks took his advice. After a couple of weeks, the tree started producing extra pitch, which pushed the beetle larvae out through holes in the bark. The tree is still going strong today.

As gardeners and maintainers of your landscapes, the best thing you can do to stave off pests and disease is maintain a healthy environment for your trees and plants through watering, fertilizing, weeding, cleaning up debris, etc., and by choosing healthy and appropriate plants and trees from the start. You may still encounter some pests or disease in your landscape, but the likelihood of major damage to your plants and trees will be greatly diminished.

Some of the most common pests and diseases we have here in Central Oregon are black spot fungus, powdery mildew, tent caterpillars, aphids, leaf miners, mites and mistletoe. Here are some suggestions that have worked for me:

If you have black spot fungus or powdery mildew, check your irrigation system. The water should be going mainly to the roots of your plants and trees. Water that is sprayed on the foliage keeps leaves damp, which can promote fungus. Certain types of trees, like aspen, are prone to black spot fungus. Sarah is not a big fan of chemicals, but for fungus she has not yet found a good alternative to fungicide. A good systemic fungicide sprayed in spring when the leaves are first coming out on the trees is usually effective to prevent black spot. If you notice spots on the leaves of your aspen later in the year, or on your smaller plants for that matter, use the same treatment. Powdery mildew, which looks like fuzzy white fur or fuzzy white spots, can be treated the same way.

Tent caterpillars are easy to spot because they weave a tent out of spider web-like material around one or more branches. Before long, you'll notice the tent crawling with small fuzzy caterpillars. Trim off the portion of the branch with the tent and dispose of it, and then put on a pair of gardening gloves and pick off any remaining caterpillars by hand and dispose of them as well. You may also spray the tree or shrub with insecticidal soap to discourage re-infestation.

Insecticidal soap is mild and non-toxic to plants and animals, and is also effective against leaf miners. Leaf miners eat the majority of the leaf leaving only a skeleton of the leaf behind. In Central Oregon they are most problematic on the Siberian Elm and can leave whole trees full of skeletonized leaves.

For aphids and mites, Sarah is a firm believer in biological control. Ladybugs are the best for getting rid of aphids and it's fun to watch them grow fat in the process. Lace-wings are also good at reducing the aphid population; the lace-wing larvae eat the aphids and the adults eat the sticky honey dew the aphids secrete on the leaves. Mites can be controlled by another type of mite called a predator mite. These predator mites eat the regular mites and when those are gone they eat each other. The praying mantis is another good garden insect that eats a variety of garden pests. If you want to know more about biological pest control and where to obtain these and other beneficial insects, consult the Resources Section in the back of this book.

Mistletoe in Central Oregon is most often found on junipers. A parasite, it looks like a bright green ball on a branch and will, over the course of many years, suck the life out of its host. On a very infected tree, you'll see many balls of mistletoe on many of the branches. At this point there is little that can be done to save the tree. If there are only one or two balls of mistletoe on the tree, the affected branches can be removed, but that doesn't guarantee that the mistletoe will not recur.

I have mentioned only a few of the common pests and diseases that can affect your landscape plants. If you have an infected plant and are unable to diagnose the problem or find a solution for it, a good place for answers is the Oregon State University Plant Clinic located at the fairgrounds in Redmond, as well as in Madras and Prineville. The clinic, where Sarah served many hours as part of her training to become a Master Gardener, is staffed by Master Gardener volunteers. Their advice service is free to the public. You need only bring a sample of the infected plant or insect pest, and they will identify it for you and recommend an appropriate treatment. We have also included the information for the plant clinic in the Resource Section at the back of this book.

When the temperature starts to drop in the fall, the pests drop off as well. So do the gardening tasks. During the next three months, you will spend most of your time preparing your landscape for winter.

Much like spring, fall is also a time for cleaning up your yard. Deadhead your flowers, trim back the dead material from your perennials, remove annuals, prune your evergreens, rake leaves, etc. By doing your cleanup now, you'll avoid a mess in the spring and an eyesore in the coming months.

If you have spring-blooming bulbs, most of these should be planted in the fall. Just follow the directions on the bag for planting depth, and mix in some good compost with your soil. This will get them off to a good start in the spring.

By late October to mid-November, you'll want to make sure that your garden is tucked away for the winter. Your trees and shrubs need fertilizing and a good final deep watering. This will get them through the winter in good shape, and give the roots the food they need to send out new growth next spring. Mulching helps protect tender plants from winter cold. You can use the leaves you raked or grass clippings as mulch over small roses and perennials and around the base of newly-planted trees and shrubs. Large rose bushes may need to be covered with protective containers, available at your local garden store.

Once your plants are tucked away, you need to winterize your irrigation system. To prevent freezing water from cracking the pipes, the water in the pipes needs to be blown out. Most landscape maintenance companies provide this service. Unless you have an air compressor, this is not a do-it-yourself proposition. Expect to pay between thirty-five and sixty dollars unless your yard is huge. This should be done by the end of October.

Now your landscape is ready for its winter hibernation. You, on the other hand, can enjoy the holiday season, knowing that your yard won't require anything from you for a few months to come.

On the other hand, if you're considering installing a new landscape, your work has probably just begun. Our last chapter will help ensure that you get off on the right foot and then make it happen.

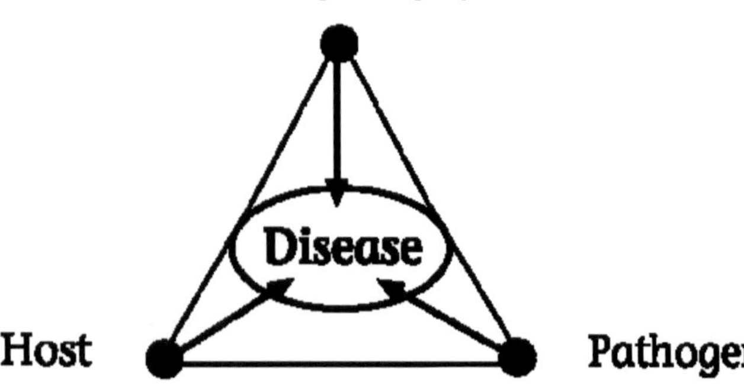

Pathology Triangle

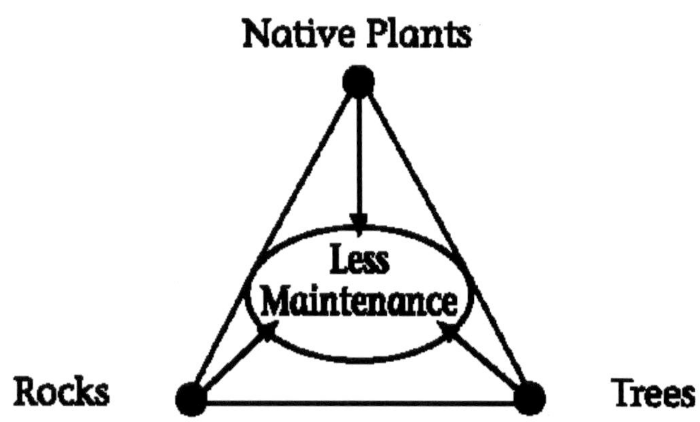

Low Maintenance Landscape

PART 3

MAKING IT HAPPEN

Chapter 10

Getting Started

The best landscape experiences flow from the best decisions. Use this chapter as a decision-making tool for your landscaping. You can participate in three ways. First go through and answer the Value by Design questions. Next, simply answer *yes* or *no* to a few thought-provoking action questions regarding contractors, bids and budget. Published ten years ago and updated here, these sets of questions have helped hundreds of people streamline their landscaping process and obtain terrific results.

55 Myths, Tips and Secrets isn't meant to be a text book. It's an insider's view of an often over-simplified and misunderstood subject, namely landscaping here in Central Oregon. With this knowledge, you'll be able to plan and maintain a landscape that will bring you joy for years to come.

It all starts with determining what you want and what you have to work with. By thoughtfully answering the questions in these few pages that follow, you'll develop a Value by Design mindset.

Tip *It's the process of design that's important.*

Our culture over-hypes, over-markets and goes over the top with over-zealous salespeople. It's no different in the landscape business. For those not in the know, ads and salesmen can create confusion. In this section you'll get an objective perspective about what's really involved and required for success.

We all want a bargain. But the other half of the deal is to get high impact for your money. Focus on the most important local aspects of landscaping. Results follow decisions. Get your thoughts and ideas down on paper. Even if you're going to design on a computer, organizing and planning requires pen and paper. As we've stressed in this book, the actual planning process is usually underrated, while pictorial plans are probably taken a little too seriously. The important thing is to work through the whole process and arrive at a thoughtfully designed response to your unique landscaping opportunities and challenges.

No one builds a house by themselves; the same applies to designing and building a landscape. It's a team effort involving owners, suppliers and workers. Most owners don't have the advantage that experience gives suppliers and contractors. But the requisite knowledge is there for the taking.

This book—and especially the questions at the end of this section—provides you with the input you need to get on track. Once you've determined what your game plan is, you may very well decide to do some of the work yourself. In fact, tapping into your skills, hobbies and imagination will give you more "skin in the game." Your participation and enthusiasm will raise the level of the result. In the context of the three main elements—people, place, and principles—

your contribution is essential. A balanced approach is the best route to success. The one-size-fits-all mentality shows up when customers give away too much control to their contractor and don't end up getting what they want.

On the other hand, you don't want to get carried away. Too many people allow their imaginations to get the best of them, forgetting that there is a difference between a colorful vision (or photograph) and an installed product that must conform to the site's features, as well as to the budget. These folks don't end up happy either.

The key to getting the best results is to balance the three elements of people, place and proven principles. If you put together an experienced team of contractors and suppliers and do your own homework, you are more than halfway there. Then use the seven secrets to put all this in perspective. An 80/20 mindset will help frame your decisions more effectively.

Tip *Use an 80/20 mindset and you'll stay focused on what is vital.*

The Value by Design process is based on this 80/20 principle, which we discussed in Chapters 1 and 4. After years in the seminar business where people are looking for advantages and innovations to give them a competitive edge, we believe the 80/20 principle is the best of the best. The idea has been written about and used for over a hundred years, but only in about the last twenty has it become well known. The formula doesn't have to be exactly 20 to 80. It could be 4 percent to 96 percent. The numbers don't really matter. The point is to concentrate your efforts on the cream of the crop. A lifelong martial artist may have many moves, but he still gets the most punch out of just a handful of techniques. In the same way, you'll get more bang for your landscape buck and have a better experience with your project, if you use this book's seven secrets, which embody the strategic 80/20 mindset.

Tip *If you want more on this 80/20 subject, read books by Brian Tracy, Stephen Covey, Peter Drucker or Richard Koch. You may also want to get a copy of Fred's book* Do Less Live Now – The Simple Success System that Never Fails *coming in 2008.*

Creating a great landscape takes preparation, vision and hard work. It may not turn out perfectly the first time around. Don't get discouraged. Edison is said to have failed 10,000 times on his way to "discovering" the light bulb. It took him even longer to figure out how to deliver the electricity to consumers. Edison succeeded because he went beyond a merely brilliant idea and figured out how his invention would be implemented. Thankfully, landscaping won't be as hard; but don't oversimplify it either.

Just because you—or a professional you hire—has plenty of experience doesn't necessarily mean that the job is being done right. Fred attended a pond-building seminar several years before water features became popular. The instructor impressed the class with the fact that he had built over 200 ponds—no small task! Then he dropped the bombshell; he admitted that he'd built ALL of them wrong. The filtration and algae problems that showed up over time were massive.

You're not going to invent the light bulb or build 200 flawed landscape ponds, but with the little bit of coaching and planning provided in this chapter, you'll wind up with better results at less emotional, physical and monetary expense.

With the Value by Design questionnaire that follows, you don't have to start at the beginning of the learning curve, even if landscaping is new to you. So enjoy the process as you start filling in your answers to these time-tested questions.

Value by Design

Secret #1 *Take a problem-solving approach.*

1. What main problem needs solving?

2. What other challenges need attention?

3. What will you eliminate?

4. What needs to be communicated to your team?

5. What neighboring features aren't appealing?

6. What else needs to be considered?

Secret #2 *Recognize value. Seize opportunities.*

1. What do you want to create?

2. Which spaces are most important?

3. How long will you live on or own the property?

4. What assets or features does the site have?

5. What is the biggest opportunity for the project?

6. What criteria will you use to measure the success of your project?

Secret #3 *Design is discovery.*

1. List important things that exist on-site now.

2. What history or nature does the place have?

3. What aspects and character need preserving?

4. Have you located all utilities?

5. Who will live in the house and use the space? What's important to them vis-à-vis your landscape?

6. What views, resources and features can be exploited in the design?

Secret #4 *Invest in a great entry.*

1. Rate your current curb appeal from 0 to 10.

2. What space do you pass as you enter the house?

3. What factors cue people to find the front door?

4. What is the experience of leaving the house?

5. How can you create interest and make your entry inviting?

6. Can you take a spectacular photo of the entry?

Secret #5 *Build outdoor rooms.*

1. What do you like to do outside your house?

2. What habits, hobbies or skills do you have?

3. What groups or events will use the space?

4. What activities require hardscapes? Which require natural treatments?

5. What might you add later?

6. How can you enhance the flow from inside the house out into the landscape or invite nature in?

Secret #6 *Unify—create a sense of place.*

1. Are the proportions and composition balanced?

2. How can you tie into the natural surroundings?

3. Can you use angles, curves and asymmetry?

4. Does the building feel like it fits the site?

5. What isn't finished yet?

6. What distracts your eye?

Now that you've answered the questions, go back using the 80/20 principle and circle in each of the six sections the one answer that jumps out at you as the most important. Then transfer these vital few concerns to the checklist on the next page. Focus on these vital few as you work your way through the design and installation of your landscape. After you have completed your 80/20 check list, please date it for your future reference. Then go on to the action checklist.

We hope you've gained insights from reading and working with all the myths, tips and secrets in our book. We've learned from writing it and doing local talks and classes since we learn from you. It's funny that we are all students and teachers for one another, often in ways we don't expect. Sometimes the biggest discoveries come from anomalies, those unexpected results, the "what's wrong with this picture" moments that reveal important insights. Keeping an open mind allows for life-long learning and enriches our lives in the process.

Working and being out in nature can literally even heal. Horticultural therapies are used with great success in rehabilitating people from injuries or illnesses. Nature helps us mentally as well. The astronauts on space lab grow plants to relieve stress. Simply going for a walk in nature can reinvigorate and inspire.

This book is meant to clear out some of the obstacles that can get in the way of that wonderful experience. We wish you great success with your landscaping efforts and enjoyment of both the process and the result!

80/20 Check List

#1 Main Problem

#2 Value Focus

#3 Discovery

#4 Entry

#5 Outdoor Room

#6 Unify

Date:

Action – Contractor Checklist

1. Do you need a subcontractor, a general contractor or both?

2. Are you getting a bid from a specialist?

3. What is the contractor's most outstanding skill (boulders, water, lighting, etc.)?

4. Is he or she a skilled craftsman or a better salesman?

5. Have you checked the landscape board website for current license and bond?

6. Is this someone with whom you want a financial relationship?

7. Do you understand the difference between a contractor and an employee?

8. Is it easy to reach prospective contractors and do they reply quickly to your messages?

9. Does your prospective contractor arrive to meetings on time?

10. Have you explored contractor referrals from friends, builders, architects, realtors, etc.?

11. Have you seen examples of the contractor's past or current jobs?

12. Will this contractor or business be around later to fix any potential problems?

Bids Checklist

1. Is this a complete project bid?

2. What is not included that will need to be done?

3. If you are comparing bids on price only, are you really looking at apples and apples?

4. Is the total fixed or is the bid for time and materials?

5. Are there clauses in the bid for up-charges? (The most typical one is the rock clause.)

6. If you and the contractor sign, are you both contractually bound?

7. Does the pay-out schedule hold back some funds until satisfactory completion?

8. Is there a completion date? What if it's not met?

9. Does the bid fit your project or is it just a generic form?

10. Are you hiring a company or a person?

11. Does the bid itemize materials and parts?

12. Is the bid too long and confusing for you to know what you are signing?

Budget Checklist

1. Do the bid and the budget match?

2. Is your budget realistic?

3 What is your Plan B if you go over budget?

4. Have you figured price per square foot for the project's area?

5. Use 10 percent of your home's value to ballpark your landscape budget.

6. How much of a fudge factor do you have for unforeseen expenses?

7. Have you included everything you want in the bid?

8. Can you compare similar projects others have recently done?

9. What quality level and features do you need?

10. Does the project need to be done at one time or can it be done in stages?

11. Have you considered different financing options?

12. Will the length of time you live there affect the budget?

Myths, Tips & Secrets Index

Bonus Myth #7

Gardening is the same as landscaping.
Landscapes without plants are empty, but plants without landscapes (a context) are not possible. While thorough knowledge of plant biology is very important, don't leave out the "bones of the landscape." The alchemy of geology, nature, and building structures all need consideration in design.

Bonus Myth #8

B-1 is the miracle supplement
B-1 is a plant vitamin already in good compost and does nothing compared to much more powerful supplements like compost tea, *Mycorrhizae fungus* or fertilizers.

Bonus Myth #9

Manzanita need to be planted using a compass
Manzanita, along with several other local natives, are surprisingly hard to transplant for a variety of reasons, none of which involve the direction in which they're planted. Plants orient toward the sunshine naturally.

Tip *Quick fixes usually lead to more problems.*
[See page 25]

Tip *Responding to the unique features of your site is a proven method to create value in your landscape. Knowing your own needs and expectations is another.*
[See page 26]

Tip *A fair number of contractors have more skill at selling than at doing a good job on your project, and the best contractors are in high demand, so choose wisely.*
[See page 28]

Tip *Landscape construction needs to account for the changing landscape!*
[See page 31]

Tip *Look around and see what's working in other landscapes.*
[See page 33]

Tip *Hours spent simply looking at—and just walking around—your site as you plan can be some of your most productive design time.*
[See page 39]

Tip *Trying to do the exact same design that you like someplace else is often misguided because your landscape isn't someplace else.*
[See page 41]

Tip *By trying to copy another landscape, you are forgetting to solve and respond to the problems unique to you and your place.*
[See page 41]

Tip *Preparation creates knowledge and knowledge improves results.*
[See page 42]

Tip *The price you pay for a car is similar to what a landscape will cost you.*
[See page 46]

Tip *Your entry, which extends from the public street or road to your front door, sells you and your house.*
[See page 50]

Tip *The price per square foot for outside living space is usually less than 5 percent of interior space.*
[See page 51]

Tip *Just because you can do something doesn't mean you should do it!*
[See page 57]

Tip *Don't hire a specialist for a manager and don't hire a generalist for features such as masonry, stamped concrete or other craftsman-level projects.*
[See page 59]

Tip *Call for existing utility locates before you start construction; various utility companies will come out and mark the locations of your existing lines.*
[See page 62]

Tip *Use a free site plan.*
[See page 62]

Tip *Mark the utility conduits as you put them in, so you can find them later.*
[See page 62]

Tip *Keep a simple list of contractors and supplier phone numbers handy.*
[See page 63]

Tip *Your site's grade needs to provide a platform for the yard's activities and construction.*
[See page 64]

Tip *Most excavators usually do flat work and install utility mains for developments, but sometimes their services are needed for big rock and material logistics on landscapes.*
[See page 64]

Tip *If you want to keep dust down use mulch, not compost (mulch retards grass or weed growth, compost promotes it).*
[See page 66]

Tip *The native grasses of our high desert ecosystem require little water and are thus drought tolerant.*

[See page 67]

Tip *You'll also want to use gravel and sand as a base underneath paver patios.*
[See page 68]

Tip *Keep in mind that built in the right place and in the right way, a water feature can mask road noise.*
[See page 69]

Tip *Here in Central Oregon our soil is usually so dry that after you remove the dirt from the hole it is a good idea to fill the hole with water. Let the water absorb into the dirt forming the hole for a few minutes. That way it will stay moister longer and when the roots start to grow out and the surrounding soil will not be so hard.*
[See page 83]

Tip *If the root ball feels loose or unstable, you may leave the ball tied at the top for up to six months. That will give the roots a chance to begin growing into the surrounding soil and the tree or plant a chance to stabilize. You still must remove the strings eventually or they will constrict the growth of the trunk and the tree will suffer.*
[See page 85]

Tip *Trees with tap roots must be root pruned and allowed to recover in the ground by growing more lateral and fibrous roots in order to transplant successfully. Assuming you've root pruned in the fall, your tree will be ready for transplanting the next spring.*
[See page 98]

Tip *Because lateral roots are closer to the surface they are more likely to be damaged by construction, herbicides, pesticides and lawn maintenance equipment. To keep your trees healthy and alive, give the roots of large trees adequate room when planning your landscape and make room for existing trees when excavating for construction.*
[See page 98]

Tip *Never put more than two to three inches of bark or mulch around the base of trees and plants. Soil balanced with air, water, and organic material including soil microbes creates healthy well-functioning roots.*
[See page 99]

Tip *Young trees have very thin bark that is easily scraped or chewed through by deer and rodents. If the cambium layer is damaged around more than half the circumference of the trunk, the production of xylem and phloem and the flow of nutrients and energy will be so compromised that the tree will die.*
[See page 100]

Tip *Around here, water is usually the ingredient that goes missing or falls short of the adequate amount. If hand-watering, use Soil Moist granules to help your trees and plants retain moisture in between waterings.*
[See page 101]

Tip *Evergreens especially should never be pruned during warm months when their sap is flowing, because flowing sap entices pestilent moths to lay their eggs on the trees. Their larvae—boring grubs—eat into the tree under the bark, causing damage to the tree.*
[See page 106]

Tip *A good rule of thumb for these kinds of shrubs is that if the flowers come before the leaves, they are blooming on last year's growth. If the flowers come after the leaves, they are blooming on this season's growth.*
[See page 106]

Tip *The only reason not to remove suckers is if you want to turn a single trunk into a clump or multiple. In some trees like Aspen or Birch, the clump is a natural tendency of the tree and may be desirable. If this is the case, keep two to three of the most substantial shoots and remove all others.*
[See page 107]

Tip *You don't have to carry a protractor with you; just make a peace sign with your first two fingers. If the crotch angel is narrower than that, the branch should be removed.*
[See page 108]

Tip *Clearing away debris like branches needles and leaves from the base of trees reduces infestation from pests and disease, and minimizes damage to the tree and surrounding soil should a fire occur.*
[See page 112]

Tip *Wearing dishwashing gloves works well for cleaning up your ornamental grasses. The rubber grips the dead grass more easily than cloth gloves, which let more dead grass slip through your grip.*
[See page 123]

Tip *When seeding wildflowers and native grasses, mix the seed in with good compost, then spread it and lightly rake it in to the soil. This gives the seed a little coverage and provides good material that will encourage germination and growth.*
[See page 123]

Tip *Another treatment for lawn rejuvenation is to spread some good compost over your lawn and rake it in. This will improve the soil for the roots, provide beneficial microbes and nutrients and even protect your lawn from turf fungus. You can*

also throw compost and turf seed into any bare spots on your lawn this time of year.
[See page 125]

Tip *It's the process of design that's important.*
[See page 137]

Tip *Use an 80/20 mindset and you'll stay focused on what is vital.*

[See page 139]

Tip *If you want more on this 80/20 subject, read books by Brian Tracy, Stephen Covey, Peter Drucker or Richard Koch. You may also want to get a copy of Fred's book* Do Less Live More – The Simple Success System that Never Fails *coming in 2008.*
[See page 140]

Secret #1 *Take an 80/20 problem-solving approach.* [See page 22]

Secret #2 *Recognize value. Seize opportunities.* [See page 30]

Secret #3 *Discover what you're working with.* [See page 35]

Secret #4 *Invest in a great entry.* [See page 48]

Secret #5 *Build outdoor rooms.* [See page 49]

Secret #6 *Unify—create a sense of place.* [See page 51]

Secret #7 *Planting recipe: Dig the hole twice as wide as the root mass (container or ball and burlap) and slightly deeper. Soak the hole with water. Drop in your tree or plant, and sprinkle Mycorrhizae fungus around the roots. Fill in around the root mass with a 50-50 mixture of compost and dirt. If the tree or plant is not on automatic irrigation, build a damn so waterings will soak deep into the roots. Lightly sprinkle fertilizer on top of the ground to jumpstart the plant. Later add compost or compost tea (a liquid form of compost). Most losses happen in the first year, so be sure to protect new trees from pests (deer, gophers, rabbits, etc...).* [See page 78]

Our Recommendations for Ideas, Help and Supplies

Ideas

Adult education COCC classes
Visit High Desert Museum
Hike Pilot, Lava, or Black Butte
Drop by the downtown library and historical society
Go to Shevlin, Drake or Pioneer Park
Walk the Bill Healy bridge river trail
Do the art hop downtown every first of the month
Attend summer master gardener or builder's tour

Help

Excavation contractors
Construction business
Landscapers
Landscape architects and designers
Real estate for referrals or locations
Chamber of Commerce
Knott Landfill and Recycling

Local Resources

Biological pest control and beneficial insects

www.Marchbiological.com
www.LadiesInRed.com

Plant disease diagnosis and treatment information

OSU Plant Clinic 548-6088

Education: classes, tours

Master Gardener training, seminars, garden tours
548-6088
Central Oregon Home & Garden Show
389-1058

Pamphlets

"Fire-Resistant Plants for Oregon Home Landscapes"
"An Introduction to Xeriscaping in the High Desert"
548-6088
"Cold Climate Gardening"
Linda Stephenson 536-2049

Home Composter

reSource 388-3638

Landscape Drawings

Tanya Carlsen 610-6961

Entomologist

Glenn Bissell 389-4942
www.alpinepest.com

Building materials
Backstrom Builders Center 382-6861

Rock: boulders, flagstones, pavers
Empire Stone Co. 617-9711

Bark, mulch, compost, sod
Instant Landscape 389-9663

Tree and plant care products, fertilizers, seed
Round Butte Seed Company 385-7001

Professional landscape parts and supplies
Horizon 382- 9333
Ewing 317-9531
Searing Plumbing and Electric 389-4618

Plants: annuals, perennials, herbs, groundcovers and grasses
Schilling Solar City Gardens 388-4680

Conservation
www.carbonfootprint.com

Landscaping
Sculptural Landscapes 382-5188

Trees and Shrubs
Bend Pine Nursery 312-9834

High Desert Garden Design Specialist
David Vala, Landscape Architect
www.Vala-Christensen.com

Trees To Go by Sarah Whipple

"Trees To Go" makes beautifying your landscape as easy as picking up the phone. First, we provide on-site evaluation and plant selection guidance. Next, if you don't have time to come to us, we'll simply pick out the trees, and then deliver and plant them for you. You can transform your yard without ever leaving home.

We have a wide selection of both deciduous and evergreen trees and shrubs, with prices as low as $5. Our planting service includes compost, fertilizer, rooting compound, and a one-year guarantee for all trees or plants on an irrigation system. Feel free to call Sarah for tree and plant recommendations. She hand-picks her inventory, guarantees it and can look at your site for FREE.

Bend Pine Nursery □ "Trees To Go"

Call now – 312-9834

Bend Pine Nursery got its start in the early nineties. The Forest Service's old Bend Pine Nursery on Deschutes Market Road was selling the last of its bare-root Ponderosa seedlings before shutting down. We planted some 30,000 seedlings and moved them up to fully-rooted container stock. We also sold wholesale contorta, aspen and other local alpines. We have specialized in native and hardy trees and shrubs best-suited to thrive in our area ever since. In 2007, we moved to our seventh Bend neighborhood – a perfect spot this time at 19019 Baker Road in Deschutes River Woods. Come visit!

Design Consultations by Fred Swisher

If your landscape project has you stuck and frustrated and you're not sure what to do next, consider a consultation session with Fred. Bringing in a neutral outside expert to look in on your project can help in several ways. It can prevent you from making big mistakes, it almost always simplifies the process and it will help generate more options and ideas. Most importantly it's a form of insurance that just might save you days of fruitless effort and thousands of dollars.

Take advantage of Fred's decades of experience. His fee in the Bend area is still just $159.00, and he guarantees that if the consultation is not worth more than twice that fee to you, it's FREE. He will visit you at your site, spend over an hour with you, and then leave you with a customized strategy in the form of a simple flow chart. He can give you estimates, connect you with suppliers and refer you to specialty contractors as well.

Both Sarah and Fred are happy to answer your questions by phone for free. If you come up with a question that neither of them can answer (it happens, but only rarely), they can refer you to an expert in that area.

"Your landscape problem solved."

Call now – 382-5188

Bibliography

Benvie, Sam. *The Encyclopedia of North American Trees*. Buffalo, New York: Firefly Books, 2002.

Bird, Richard. *Garden Answers Pruning.* London: Hamlyn, 2002.

Campbell, Frederick C. and Dubé L. *Landscaping Makes Cents*. Pownal: Vermont: Storey Communications, Inc., 1997.

Editors. *Complete Guide to Trees & Shrubs*. Des Moines, Iowa: Meredith Books.

Editors. *Sunset Western Garden Book.* Menlo Park, California: Sunset Publishing Corporation, 1998.

Editors. *Sunset Western Garden Problem Solver.* Menlo Park, California: Sunset Publishing Corporation, 1998.

Johnsen, Jan and Fech, John C. *All About Trees.* Des Moines, Iowa: Meredith Books, 1999.

Hagender, Fred. *The Meaning of Trees.* San Francisco, California: Chronicle Books, 2005.

Lang, Susan and editors. *Bonsai.* Menlo Park, California: Sunset Publishing Corporation, 2003.

Lowenfels, Jeff and Lewis, Wayne. *Teaming with Microbes: A Gardener's Guide to the Soil Food Web.* Portland, Oregon: Timber Press, 2006.

Pakenham, Thomas. *Remarkable Trees of the World,* New York: W.W. Norton & Company.

Petrides, George A. and Petrides, Olivia. *Field Guide to Western Trees.* South New York: Houghton Mifflin Co., 1992.

Roberts, Jonathan. *Mythic Woods.* London: Weidenfeld & Nicolson, 2004.

Rushforth, Keith. *The Easy Tree Guide.* London: Duncan Petersen Publishing, 2004.

Tomlinson, Harry. *101 Essential Tips Bonsai.* London: Dorling Kindersley Limited, 1996.

Trudge, Colin. *The Tree.* New York: Crown Publishers, 2005.

Water, Denver. *Xeriscape Plant Guide*. Golden, Colorado: Fulcrum Publishing, 1996.

Notes